I Think

God Likes Me

Discovering God as your Counterpart

by

Yan G. Venter.

Published by
YVM Books
2426 Crow Mountain Rd
Russellville, AR 72802
USA

Unless otherwise indicated, all Scripture quotations are taken from the Amplified version of the Bible.

First published in the USA in November 2003 by Yan Venter Ministries
Second print in February 2013, by YVM Books

For information address:
YVM Books, 3426 Crow Mountain Rd, Russellville, AR 72802, USA.

Table Of Contents

Introduction

Anytime I choose to read a book, the writer must immediately convince me that he has a good understanding of the subject, and furthermore, he must dwell at the level where I find myself, or at least entice me to come up to the level where I am supposed to be.

This book is not intended for academic purposes, but is most definitely prepared for those who have a desire to discover the realm of the spirituals.

After serving God for more than forty years, I guess I can say without fear of contradiction that I have seen both sides of the spectrum.

I have dwelt amongst the Academic Clan and I have listened to all they have to say. Some have been great, while others were just outright boring. I have completed my share of studies and enjoy reading on a great variety of subjects. The doctrines of man and the rifts amongst organizations has never really interested me, and I have almost concluded that just about everyone is wrong here or there. However, they are too proud to admit it, and refuse to correct themselves for fear of admitting to being human.

Except for only a few countries of the world, I have had the honor of visiting most, and my eyes have admired the grandeur and beauty of most of the impressive sites, this planet have to offer.

Nothing in my life, have been so impressive, as discovering and living in the realm of the spirituals. Walking with God, and not just faking it to impress others.

If there is something I hate more than sin itself, then it is when I find myself trying to fake this walk or to bluff others about being where I am not.

Life is full of struggles and challenges. The idea is definitely to keep your focus and complete the race successfully that is set before us.

Hypocrisy is not an option and worshipping something or someone who cannot fill this place in your heart, must be avoided at all costs.

Once your spirit has tasted the real, true water of life, you cannot and should not allow anything else to replace it. In fact, nothing can take its place, but I have arrived at moments, where all of a sudden, you "wake up" and say, "where am I, or what am I doing?" You are not where you are supposed to be, and you are involved with the religious and all their outward appearances and empty cliché's, but the warm embrace of your Lord is no longer felt.

This happens, and when it does, God will have to help you because that "stuff" rubs off on you and believe me, it sticks like glue.

In the bible, repeatedly we find God saying, *"Consider your ways and set your mind on what has come to you. You have sown much, but you have reaped little; you eat, but you do not have enough; you drink, but you do not have your fill; you clothe yourselves, but no one is warm."*[1]

Yes, something is wrong, drastically wrong, and the answer lies between you and God. No great revelation is necessary. You don't need any prophet or great expounder of truth to bring you the answer. Neither do you need to lie on the Psychiatrists couch and let him test his secular skills on your spirit man.

No, the answer is within your own heart. You know where it all started. You know where the moment arrived when you compromised your love for Him and a double mindedness entered your heart and left you with the role of Jackal and Mr. Hyde.

God instructed the prophet to go to the priests and ask them to decide this question of law:

1   If one carries in the skirt of his garment flesh that is holy [because it has been offered in sacrifice to God], and with

---

[1] Haggai 1:5-6

his skirt or the flaps of his garment he touches bread, or pottage, or wine, or oil, or any kind of food, does what he touches become holy [dedicated to God's service exclusively]? And the priests answered, No! [*Holiness is not infectious.*]

2. Then said Haggai, if one who is [ceremonially] unclean because he has come in contact with a dead body should touch any of these articles of food; shall it be [ceremonially] unclean? And the priests answered, it shall be unclean. [*Unholiness is infectious.*][1]

In the circles of the church, we do rub shoulders with those who unfortunately do not have the same hunger, or sincerity to live for their Lord as you do.

This statement is not meant to sound like mere criticism, and if it does, I apologize, but there is no other way to say it. I have had my share of religion, and I have been on the mountain with God. The mountain is better.

In October of 2,000, my friend, Pastor Cleddie Keith, from Florence Kentucky, invited me to a meeting where Evangelist Rodney Howard Browne, was ministering. I thought the meeting was pretty good although I was not very impressed with some of the "semantics" that took place during the altar service. I did not say anything to anyone about it, as I was raised never to criticize the man of God, but I was trying to see what it was that were drawing people to a service that was so unlike any "normal," or proper service. I wanted to find out what it was that drew people to a meeting that did not fulfill to any of the regular Clerical conditions.

I remember that I liked the glow in the young preachers face, and was impressed with the warmness of his spirit as he allowed himself to be used by God.

Suddenly, I remembered that this is exactly where I used to be, but that I have allowed the "unclean spirit of religion" to rub off on me.

---

[1] Hag 2:11-13

The following night I invited my pastor, John Swint, together with several others to attend the next meeting with me. On the way to church, I tried to "inform" them about some of the things this preacher would be doing during the altar service.

"Last night, the man put his foot on the belly of a man whom he was praying for while the man was laying on his back," I said, trying to prepare them for what was coming. Laughter broke out in the car, and I was surprised to find that mine hat a touch of nervousness to it.

"Now what will you do if he were to do it to you?" Pastor Swint was jokingly asking, not realizing that this would be exactly where God would have me in just a couple of hours later.

With the house of God almost full of people, my wife and I responded when the man of God called us forward for prayer. The Spirit of God came over both of us like a flood, and I found myself lying on the floor and enjoying every moment of it.

With the foot of the preacher, resting firmly on my belly, I realized how hungry I was. I realized how long it has been since I was at the place where He would feel comfortable enough to visit with me. This great friend of mine and I, have somehow separated and only now, on the floor, did it dawn on me.

Oh, I remember clearly how right it felt, when both my wife and I broke out in a demonstration of freedom and an expression of intimacy.

It felt so right to drop "the bucket" of religion and pretence that was handed to me by the company of those who expected you to join them in carrying the mere waters of the realm of the mortals.

It felt so right to allow the wells of salvation to break free from my innermost belly, knowing that this is really what it is all about. Nothing more and nothing less!

Since then, I have been telling people that in the year 2000 "I got born-again, again."

This, dear Reader, is what this book is all about. Focusing on what is real and majoring on the majors.

Remember the words of Peter, after he discovered the real essence of God's Spirit, when he said, "Repent (*change your mind and purpose*); turn around and return [*to God*], that your sins may be erased (*blotted out, wiped clean*), that times of refreshing (*of recovering from the effects of heat, of reviving with fresh air*) may come from the presence of the Lord."[1]

Whatever there may be about us now, dear Reader, which is not what we feel it ought to be, let the call of God come to each one of us at this moment, "Set thine house in order."

Repentance brings us back into relationship. Not the vain regrets, in which we sometimes indulge.

> *"Repentance is to leave*
> *The sins we loved before,*
> *And show that we in earnest grieve*
> *By doing so no more."*

For us to have any real relationship with our Lord, we must make sure that our house is set in order!

If you dare, turn the page now, and allow me to share with you about what is real. While you are reading, ask God to change in you, what need to be change.

---

[1] Acts 3:19 AMP

Chapter One

There is a loving, holy fear, which is never cast out. Filial fear grows as love grows. That sacred dread, that solemn awe of God, we must ever cultivate; but we are not afraid of Him. Dear heart, God is your best Friend, your choicest love.
"Yea, mine own God is he,"[1]

I think God likes me, Dad.

Life was very normal for me until God showed up in my life. The only problem was this; I had no idea that this was God who showed up in my room.

I was only twelve years old and knew nothing about God. To me, God was only someone who lived in Heaven, and as far as I was concerned, He was something like a Santa Claus, or the Tooth Fairy. It was good to believe in Him when you were scared or in need of some assurance when others talked about the devil.

Church was not important to our family then. Every now and then Dad would get a desire to attend church somewhere and even then it was normally to some dead, religious situation that was a dread to me and everyone else in the home. Normally I had a hard time keeping my eyes open while the preacher carried on with his boring sermon.

---

[1] Unknown

Dad was a good man. One of the hardest workingmen I knew. Him, like so many others of his time, came through the great depression and the hard lines of tough living was clearly visible in his face. It left this good man with seriousness about life that was tough on us kids. But, he was a good man. He took care of his family.

He had a strange drive inside him of always making sure that we had enough food in the house. He never would buy food in a small way. Whenever he bought food, it was always in abundance. He never went to the butcher to buy a few pounds of lamb. No, he would go to a farmer and buy a few sheep! He never bought just a few pounds of sausage. Uh, uh, he bought a cow and a pig and made hundreds of pounds of sausage to have enough meat in the freezer for the entire winter. Whenever he wanted chicken, he would arrive at the house with a dozen live chickens. Every edible part of these animals would ultimately be eaten.

Dad would make sure of that. Yep, Dad took care of his home.

The same counted for vegetables. Dad did not believe in making flower gardens. He believed that the water had to be put to better use than that. Therefore, every available patch of land had vegetables growing in it. Even on the front porch he had beanstalks as "the pride and joy" of our family.

Yes, Dad took care of his family.

He was an honest, hard workingman, and expected the same from everyone else in the house.

He did not believe in homework after school either. School for him was a necessary evil that kept his children occupied when they could actually help earn an income. Schoolwork had to be done during school hours. As soon as you came home, your time belonged to him.

Except for boxing, Dad did not allow us any other sporting activities.

"You are born fighters, and you need to prove it," dad would always tell my brother Nick and I. At every available opportunity dad would find us someone to fight, and when there was no one around to get us into a fight with, he would match Nick and I together with each other.

"Yan is going to become the next World Champion boxer," dad would always say to the disdain of Nick who was an outstanding boxer and four years older than me.

Dad owned a mercantile factory and as we matured (He decided when you were ready) you were introduced into the factory and earned your keep. He made sure you did not work for free though. No, you earned a few dollars, but with that income you were taught to buy your own clothes or whatever you needed.

Yes, dad took care of his family.

Every afternoon dad would stop at the liquor store and purchase a half a quart of brandy. He made sure that us kids understood that he was not an alcoholic, but would not go without the brandy. He would not bother anyone, but no one should mess with him either. The children respected dad greatly, but one thing was for sure; you never joked around with dad. He was the head of the home and everyone understood that.

The day was finally over for me. I had just finished my chores around the house and was lying on my bed with school recommended reading in my hand. TV was not yet introduced into our country, and the radio played an important role in most families' lives.

Each night, the family would sit around the table and listen to our favorite story on the radio. At the end of the story, each of us had to take turns to make the late cup of coffee for our parents, and that evening was my turn.

Finally, I had a chance to retire to my room, and I was about a half an hour into my prescribed school reading when all of a sudden, the strong disciplined voice of my dad called out my name. There was no doubt in my mind that it was dad calling.

In my normal militant fashion, I threw the book down and headed straight for dad's bedroom without any delay. Dad did not like to call more than one time, and all our kids knew that too well.

"Yes, dad," I said enquiringly after showing up in the doorway of his bedroom. He was reading the daily newspaper. Dad was friendly but stern as he answered me back. "Yes, what?" He lifted his head up slightly from the pillow, as he looked at me.

"I heard you calling me dad," I said apologetically.

"No Yan," I did not call you. Go and lay down and rest." Dad's encouraging tone of voice assured me that I was making a mistake, and as I walked back to my room I was confused.

A strange fear was gripping my heart, but I tried to drown it in the book I was supposed to read, when only a few minutes later, dad's strong voice called out once more. This time it was louder than before, and I knew that I was not making a mistake.

In the same, prompt manner, I jumped out of bed and walked quickly to his room. This time my bones were shaking. I could not hold still and tears were flowing over my cheeks. For the life of me, I could not understand what was going on with me.

Dad did not allow us boys much room for crying. but now, I stood before dad and there was no way I could stop the tears. I was not ashamed about it, but I was terribly confused. Inside me, something had happened. I felt swallowed up by something big, something much larger than I have ever experienced. Dad looked up at me with an enquiring look.

"Yes, Dad?" This time I walked right up next to his bed. Tears streamed down my cheeks and I tried in vain to control myself, but was not having any success. I was shaking all over, and it was not cold.

It took only a moment to make my observation that there was no hoax involved with my dad here.

This time dad was genuinely surprised about my appearance. Mom was lying on the bed next to dad and she now lifted her head with a concerned look in her eye.

They were genuinely surprised about me coming back the second time. Dad, sat up straight, and swung his legs off the side of the bed.

"Come here son."

The tone in his voice was not the normal one. He was uncommonly tender and the look on his face gave me the assurance that it was genuinely not him who called my name.

"Yan, I really did not call you my son, but why don't you tell me what happened?" With his hand he indicated for me to sit next to him on the bed. I was shivering all over and could not understand it.

The empty bottle of brandy with the last remains of it still in the half empty glass, told me that dad was not completely sober but not drunk either. We hardly ever saw him really drunk.

Dad noticed my quick glance towards the remains in his glass and with a slight look of guilt on his face he picked up the glass, and emptied the contents down his throat. As he put the glass back on the bedside table, he looked back at me as if to say, "Now it is gone, let's get on with it."

I hated that brandy with a passion and dad knew it. All us kids hated it, but that was the last thing on my mind right now. I was so scared and I did not know why.

Teary eyed and shaking, I told dad about the way that "his voice" called me twice before and that I was not making a mistake.

"Especially this last time dad; it was very real."

What followed next, would forever stay with me. It would become a treasure in my life that no one could take away from me.

Dad reached for his bible. It was in the bedside table underneath the pile of statements and other junk. "My dad, reached for his bible!"

His strong hands paged through the book, until he found first Samuel and Chapter three. Time stood still for me as I listened, mesmerized at the similarity between the little boy Samuel, in the bible, and me.

Mom, who always seemed to have time to pray in any situation, was sitting straight up on the bed now, and she had a strange glow in her eyes.

She was the prayer warrior at home and would never give up on praying for her whole family. Many a night I would listen to her after dad had sunken into a deep "Brandy-slumber," she would be on her face, calling on Almighty God.

I would lay there and hear her call each child's name, and when she would get to my name, she would pause, often times cry and mumble a few strange words, and then she would say, "now Lord, Yan is different. I have given him to you. Please let Your will be fulfilled." I did not understand her prayers then, but now, as she stared at me with excitement written all over her face, I understood. Destiny came together, and I felt like a little Moses in a basket, ready to be pushed in amongst the weeds of time.

Dad's stern voice brought me back to reality, when he said, "now, go back to your room and this time, when you hear that voice call your name again, you fall on your face before Almighty God and do like Samuel did. Tell the Lord that you are ready to listen and then you come and tell me what happened."

Dad seemed to have all the answers, I thought. I just could not understand why he would expect me to go in there all by myself!

I could not believe what my dad was expecting me to do! "God, was actually going to come to my room, and I had to go in there as a young twelve-year old boy and wait for Him?"

Fear had come over me but dad would have it no other way. This time he spoke in his normal strict manner, and told me to leave the room and "go and wait on God." I knew that it was time to obey and I left his room without any further delay.

My room felt so small as I went back into it. My mind was racing in a dozen different directions and my heart seemed to beat at a faster pace than ever before. I felt so vulnerable but at the same time, I knew that there was nowhere to hide from God.

Looking back today, I know how incredibly awesome the moment was for that twelve year old me. "God was fixing to pay me a visit for real, and he was no longer a tooth fairy or a Santa Clause. No, He was very real, for I knew then that I already heard Him speak to me twice before."

I don't know how long I was waiting for my Lord to enter that room. No, I can't remember. But what I do remember is the moment He did enter, He spoke my name for the third time, and then, several things happened at the same time.

His voice was gentle. Very gentle! Fear departed from me and a gentle, yet also powerful presence, came over my young life. I was taken into a realm greater than this physical one. This was life like I had never felt before. This was love in the ultimate experience and I knew that I wanted to be in no other place than right there, at the feet of the Master.

His voice was real and sweet! I felt raptured into His presence and as I slipped onto my knees in front of the Master, I realized even as a little twelve-year lad that, this was where I belonged. I knew then that I wanted to be at the feet of the Master for the rest of my life.

I knew that he claimed me, the moment I heard His whisper, and when He said my name the third time.

Time did not matter to me. No one had to tell me what sentences to use, or what kind of words to apply in those moments of sweet communication. The Lord introduced Himself to me that day. No one came close to my room and until the late hours of the night I was in prayer and communication with God. I enjoyed every moment of it, and when I finally got up from my knees, I was complete. Destiny was lined out for me and I knew where I belonged.

One thing was for sure. From that moment on I was different. I was totally changed and everyone in the house would take notice of it from then on.

Early the following morning dad called me to his room. He was curious and told me to sit on the side of the bed "and tell me everything in detail."

Mom cried as I told dad about my incredible experience and the manner in which God talked to me. Each time I looked at her, there was something familiar there. I could not place it at first, but then it dawned on me! "She knew Him also! She knew the same Friend I had just met and now I felt closer to her than ever before."

Dad was only excited because as he put it, "You are a little Samuel."

I explained to them how afraid I was at first and how terrible the moment seemed to me knowing that the God of Heaven was going to pay me a visit.

I also explained to them how incredible the peace was that followed the presence of the Master and how intense His voice was as He visited with me at that very tender age.

Dad was listening intently and his eyes were open wide. Mom was crying softly, but through the tears there was a constant smile.

"What did God tell you? Dad asked me, but suddenly I realized that dad was not going to understand any of the things yet. Mom would, and later I would share more with her, but right then, I was looking for something to tell my dad that he could understand.

"Dad," I said, pausing for just a moment. "*I think God likes me*."

Dad briefly enjoyed the moment, by breaking out in laughter, but then after a while, he told me not to tell other people "God liked you."

"God does not *like* people Yan. He loves the whole world."

I nodded in agreement but realized that dad obviously did not understand, as he was not there when I felt my Lord's eyes on me. He was not there when words were whispered into my spirit.

"No, there was more than just a corporate love involved here." Later on, I would discover the favor of the Lord and how that God would choose some to call for special tasks. I did not feel myself to be more special than others and never have, but through the years, I realized that the relationship between God and myself would develop into something very special.

The way God talked to me was different. He liked me, and to tell the truth, the feeling was mutual.

I loved Him, but oh my, I liked my Lord.

I think she likes you.

Years later, the same words would once again come up when I walked into the place where my wife was working.

She was young and beautiful. She was every-thing I had been hoping for, but there was only one problem at that time. She belonged to someone else. I was told that she was about to get engaged to another man.

My sister Sienie, who was working with her at the beauty salon, told me jokingly to take my eyes off the young lady, because she was already spoken for.

I could not help but notice how her beautiful, brown eyes briefly met with mine in the mirror, but I was not going to allow myself to be drawn into a place of immoral behavior.

"If she is spoken for, then I better not pursue the matter any further," I said to myself and sadly left the Salon an hour later.

My brother-In-Law, who was visiting the salon with me, took me by the arm outside and said, "Are you leaving just like this?"

Confused, I looked at the well-meaning friend of mine and said, "She belongs to another!"

"Not yet!" he protested wildly. *"I think she likes you."*

Suddenly the words grabbed me deep down inside. "I used those words once after I met my Lord!"

"Are you sure?" I asked, coming to a sudden halt. "What gives you that idea?" I was waiting for just the right answer.

"Just the way she looked at you man. If you did not notice how she looked at you, then there is something wrong with your lookers." He giggled as he said it, but it brought a spark into me, and I turned on my heels and headed back into the salon. I walked past my sister, and right up to the pretty little girl.

"Look me in the eye Bessie,[1] and tell me if you feel the same as me right now," I said to the young, pretty lady.

I knew that there was destiny in our getting together and if it were so, we would both know it right at that moment.

She smiled at me, and nodded. Our eyes and our hearts connected and we knew without a doubt that we were meant for one another.

I told her right then, (and I know it sounds arrogant), "we belong together, and if I was you, I would not waste the other man's time nor his money on a ring."

With excitement written all over her face, she smiled and said, "OK."

After leaving the salon that day, I felt complete. My search was over. I had found my counterpart. I found my soul mate; the one with whom I wanted to share the rest of my life with.

Six months later, we were married.

To the Ephesian Church, the Apostle Paul, wrote saying, "For this reason a man shall leave his father and his mother and shall be joined to his wife, and the two shall become one flesh. This mystery is very great, but I speak concerning [the relation of] Christ and the church.[2]

The same way in which my wife showed me that her eyes were unmistakably on me, and that she preferred me above all other, is how I felt when my Lord's eyes fell on me. I was special and so was He. He was to me, like

---

[1] Her name is really Elizabeth, but her friends call her by this name.

[2] Eph 5:31-32

none other and at that moment, nothing else would serve to satisfy me

"Bold shall I stand in that great day,
For who aught to my charge shall lay?
While through thy blood absolved I am
From sin's tremendous curse and shame."

Chapter Two

"Pray for the mantle, girdle, and the blessing of Elijah, for the love of John, and the zeal of Paul, to twine hearts together to draw souls to heaven; till the Beloved comes like a roe upon the mountain of spices; till the shadows flee away, and the Day-star arise in your hearts." [1]

In A Corner And No Place for A Lie

Only one seat was still open in the full Boeing 737 Aircraft, and it was as if it was specially reserved for me.

The only problem was, that it was the one I disliked the most. Often times, the bulkhead seat in the Southwest Airlines Carriers, are arranged with two seats facing each other. One seat is arranged in such a way that you are flying backwards.

After seating myself in this uncomfortable, backward position, I became aware that one of the men opposite me was engaged in sharing the gospel with the fellow next to me.

---

[1] Samuel Lee (1625-1711)

The Christian was well "armed", and not merely religious. His eyes revealed the love of Christ and it was evident that he had a definitive, working relationship with the Lord. He was neatly dressed and displayed genuineness in his approach.

It was obvious that he was not about to relinquish his "hold" on the soul next to me, and for the next following minutes, he pursued this rebellious soul with all the effort he could muster. But this stubborn candidate had an answer to everything, or at times, even an arrogant question to shoot back at this well-meaning Christian. He tried his best to put an end to the conversation with the normal religious jargon about how good of person he was, and that he was a member of some "*First*" Church.

In my mind I compared the two men and it was obvious how different the two of them were. One, the epitome of religion, whiles the other one was filled with the genuine love of Christ.

The other fellow passengers around us were not saying anything, but I could not help but notice how even though they did not look in our direction for fear of becoming the next one in line for this passionate man of God, they were listening.

"The man is a Soul-winner for sure," I said to myself. For the next half an hour I sat and listened quietly to this drama playing itself off next to me. I was praying for Christian to get his breakthrough, but it became increasingly clear that the candidate had no plans to surrender.

"Excuse me sir," I joined in as soon as the conversation allowed for the interruption. I looked at the man next to me, and I could not help but to notice that he was rather agitated and ready to get out of this conversation as soon as possible. It was obvious that

Christian had him in a corner and would not relent on his "hold."

"Yes," the man almost barked out at me, but I was not going to be deterred, as I joined the attempt to break through this man's Jericho-like wall.

I could not help but to smile as Christian sighed a sigh of relief as he realized he now had a brother and companion on his side.

"If I was you sir," I said with emphasis, and loud enough for the others to hear: "I would pay much closer attention to what this man have to say."

A question mark formed on the candidate's forehead, and the corners of his mouth dropped down into an arrogant expression.

"Why is that?" He asked loudly with the evidence of obvious religion evident in his entire demeanor.

I could not help but notice Christian's appreciation for my moral support, and a few of the other passengers turned their heads towards us with a renewed interest as this "third-party" joined in the "struggle".

"Well," I said, stretching the word out a little longer than was necessary, before continuing. "You see sir, I am a preacher of the Gospel, and the devil hates me." I said it without a smile, and before he could find an answer or a question, I continued with my proclamation.

"The devil has tried to kill me on many an occasion. I have had a motor home go over the side of a cliff, I have had sharks attack me in the water and last year a lion tried to get me through a car window in Africa.

At this point I noticed that the people around me were openly looking in our direction, so I continued with renewed fervor.

"A while back I fell four stories from a building, while putting up a roof on a church building and died on the spot, but they prayed for me and God resurrected me from the dead. I lifted up my left arm that was still in a cast and showed him the "remains" of the last attack.

His eyes followed my arm as I lifted it up for him to get a better look at it. For the first time, the man was really quiet, and he allowed me to continue without an interruption. "Together with this arm I broke a total of forty-two bones in my body.

"Now," I said in a business-like manner, "the chances are about ninety percent Sir, that this Airplane won't land with me in it. The big question though is this: Are you ready for eternity?"

I was somehow expecting a humorous response, but instead, silence was hanging heavily over us for a few seconds. I used the moment to observe the situation around me. Some of the other passengers were literally staring at me with a worried look on their faces, while the man next to me appeared suddenly nervous. His bravado was gone and the realization that church and religion and all the good works that he repeatedly referred to, was no longer good enough.

Suddenly he appeared so vulnerable. It was evident that he was now keenly aware of his own shortcoming.

Christian was smiling. In fact, he found my story quite humorous, but at that moment when death and the thin cord of life became so real, it was obvious in whom Christ could be seen.

The absence of fear was visible in Christian, but the man who so bravely proclaimed his religious affiliations was visibly shaken.

There was no sign of humor on his face. In fact, I was surprised to see how that moment affected the candidate as well as the others that were now no longer trying to look in another direction.

Silence had fallen over the little crowd and fear was visibly present in their stare.

The false foundation that religion offered suddenly proved to be insignificant and they knew it.

The Psalmist says, "[After all] You do set the [wicked] in slippery places; You cast them down to ruin and destruction.

How they become a desolation in a moment! They are utterly consumed with terrors!

The few lines of that sweet Gospel song suddenly echoed through my spirit as I realized once again how sweet it is to have the sweet assurance that *Jesus is mine*."

"Oh, Beulah land, sweet Beulah land,
I'm longing for thee.
Beulah land, sweet Beulah land."

Suddenly the man looked back at Christian and with the same serious look still on his face, he said: "Now run all that stuff by me again will you?"

Spectacular Truth

Ever since Constantine made Christianity the official religion of the Western world, there have been an awful lot of Christians. Maybe too many! But since that time, there have been only a few believers who, above all else, have sought to know the Lord Jesus in a very personal continuing walk.

That is the way it was, that is the way it is, and that is the way it is probably going to stay ... right on up until the trumpet sounds.

If you question this assessment, then consider the following fact. It is a pretty undeniable indication that too many "Christians" are not really focused on getting to know their Lord better.

On many occasions I have stood before large groups of ministers and spoken of the need of knowing Jesus Christ intimately, and of this being the central issue in the believer's life.

I have often made the following statement: it is possible to know Jesus Christ personally, intimately, and daily. Furthermore, it is also possible to step outside of space-time, outside of this realm into the other realm, and there personally know and encounter your Lord, to worship Him and fellowship with Him there, in another realm.

Friend, you have to allow me this: That is one heavy statement. That statement begs to be challenged, accepted, or at least inquired of! For more than thirty years, I have sought to declare but one thing, the Lord Jesus Christ.

I have been "Amen-ed", I have been applauded, I have been cheered, and, yes, I have even had standing ovations, but the greatest of all

24

was when believers or ministers of the Gospel would walk up to me and say, "Show me how to step outside of space-time into that other realm and fellowship with my Lord there."

In the general sense, Christians love to be preached to, love to be swept over by the power of preaching, love to be thrilled and chilled, love to exult in what has been said, and love to go to conferences where all these wonderful things happen, but they do not enter into deep fellowship with the Lord.

Most are not really focused on getting to know their Lord better.

This however, is not just today's problem. This problem was around with yesteryear's Christians, and the day before yesterday's Christians. You can push that back all the way through the last seventeen hundred years. It has been that long since Jesus Christ was the intimate, experience-able centrality of the Christian's faith.

As a young man in his early twenties, Watchman Nee was under the tutorship of Sister Barber. One day young Nee came to Miss Barber with a very think dissertation he had written on eschatology. It was a premillennial discussion of the signs and symbols found in Daniel, Ezekiel, and Revelation. Sister Barber said to young Nee, "You do not wish to take this direction in your ministry." Her simple statement arrested Nee and his enthusiasm for speculation about the second coming of Christ.

On yet another day, this exuberant young Chinese burst into Sister Barber's house and told her that he had just heard one of the best speakers he had ever listened to. "Here is a really great Christian who knows the Lord." Said Nee. Sister Barber went with Nee to a meeting and heard the man speak. After the meeting was over she gave the following observation:

This man has a great deal of power, but internally he knows very, very little of the Lord Jesus Christ." Nee was stunned.

Sometime later, Nee came to Sister Barber's house again, full of enthusiasm. "You must hear a man I have just heard. He is filled with the Lord. This time you will really be impressed." Sister Barber once more went with Nee to hear a visiting minister who was speaking to Christians in that city. After hearing the man speak, Sister Barber had this to say. "This is a highly intelligent man. He has a brilliant understanding of the Scripture. He is a very eloquent speaker. But internally he knows very little of the Lord Jesus Christ." Again, Nee was astounded.

Sometime later, Nee once more burst into Sister Barber's home. "I found a man who really knows the Lord. Everything that he says lets you know that this man walks with the Lord Jesus.

You must come hear this godly man. I am sure this time you will agree with me."

Once more Sister Barber went with young Watchman Nee to hear a speaker. This time her observations were slightly different. Listen very carefully to her words.

"Many years ago this man had a profound experience with Jesus Christ. It was an experience that changed his life and brought brokenness into his life' but he has been living on that experience and preaching on that experience ever since. He does not have an up-to-date, present walk with the Lord. He is operating on a past encounter with God."

On this occasion something got through to Nee. You might say that Nee began to realize what few Christians do. He began to see the necessity of the importance of having a living, up-to-date, experiential relationship with Jesus Christ. All doctrine, all power, all practice, all concepts, all creeds pale into insignificance and bow to one point: The centrality of Jesus Christ in all things.[1]

Your Lord is to be experienced.

A large part of your personal relationship with Jesus Christ is supposed to be corporate and in community, not individual.

Understand this. When I speak of corporate or community, I am speaking about that which is the most holy and the most precious thing in this whole universe to your Lord. Perhaps it is not very precious to Christians today, but it is precious to God. To him, it is the most sacred element within creation. I speak of the *Ecclesia*. And the Ecclesia is not a thing; the ecclesia is a she – a bride! A visible, observable, attendable, ongoing gathering ... the body of believers, a community of the redeemed, a colony from heaven, a nation, a world within this world. Jesus Christ died for her. And it is within her that He moves, and where you are supposed to live, and in that community you are supposed to get to know Him.

Everywhere I go to minister, I am constantly aware of His presence and incredible anointing to lead, guide and instruct me, concerning the ones

---

[1] Quoted from Gene Edwards, "The Journey Inward."

whom I am entrusted with during that time of ministry.

It is within this corporate, living "Organism," that one finds the satisfaction of experiencing him as the great Shepherd and Bride Groom. It is here where you learn about his great love. Not on your own. No, right there among the ones who will ultimately become known as "his workmanship."

You cannot live this Christian life!

The other realm is unattainable unless taken there by the Spirit.

It is a real world, but invisible. It is tangible, yet untouchable. It has voices in, yet cannot be heard by mortal ear. It has living beings in and yet cannot be seen with the naked eyes.

Yes, that world, dear reader, is as real as the one you are living in right now, but it cannot be reached unless you are taken by the hand and carefully directed into its atmosphere of peace and tranquility.

That world has its own King. Our Lord!

This book is intended for those who finally can admit that you cannot live the Christian life merely on your own merits or mortal abilities. Learn that and liberation is near.

This book is intended for "failures"! The ones who finally gave up trying and the ones who will finally throw in the towel and say, "*I have had enough of not enough.*"

Like me, you have been given the "Ten Steps," and the untold "How-to-do-it," but you are still nowhere nearer to your goal of enjoying your Lord than when you started.

You are surrounded by the many who knows all the answers but around them you notice, they too don't know the intimacy of our Lord.

You have tried to do the one and two-hour prayers, and the list of things to consider, reaching from dress codes to church codes, but yet the brass ceiling has prevailed above you and you feel like a prisoner in your own mind.

Your prayer life has finally dwindled to a standstill and your bible reading has totally ended.

In fact, you have about decided to join the rest of the folks who have mastered the art of the bluff.

It doesn't make any sense to you, why in the world you stand in church each Sunday, pay your tithe and listen to one boring sermon after another without the real feeling of satisfaction. Yet, you like so many others like you, allow yourself to continue in a direction that offers very little satisfaction.

The few times when you still tried to find an answer as to why you don't feel anything at all, you were quickly silenced by the "Masters Of The Bluff," when they told you, that we don't go by feeling, we only go by faith.

Even after you were told that the answer was in the "Baptism Of The Holy Spirit", you were surprised to see how soon, even this experience wore off, and once again, you were left on the island of self destruction and at the sunset of mere religious concepts, where you definitely did not feel the love of the Lord as you should.

But, once again you were told that "where two or three are gathered in his name, He is there," but looking around you cannot help but notice that the Lord is nowhere near any of you. You have noticed the absence of relationship between them and the Lord. Finally, you decided that you would have to just admit defeat. You just cannot live this Christian life!

The demands are beyond your abilities and the rules are too far out of reach from a sinful and rebellious, carnal nature, which just cannot understand the things of the Spirit of God, because it is incapable of doing so.

It is at this point of time, when you are wearied by drawing your own water from the well of man's discovery like the woman at the well,[1] when you will discover His appearance. It is at this point where He will offer you water which will fill your innermost being.

"There are so many vices and imperfections in our nature, and we are so feeble and weak, that we have very great need daily to pray unto Him, yeah, and that more and more, that He will not suffer us to decline from His will."[2]

Only then will the scales fall from your eyes and will you experience your Lord in a way that surpasses any of the do's and don'ts of human society.

Yes, there are so many vices and imperfections in our nature, that you finally have to agree, "it is impossible to live this Christian life." You can no longer fool yourself by saying that this is not true. You have tried and tried and failure after failure almost left you at a place where you have to merely stand back, and from a distance "admire" the ones who have discovered something that you do not have.

Look back right now. Ask yourself the question, "What was I told that I am supposed to do

---

[1] John 4:4-24
[2] John Calvin (1509-1564)

to become a good Christian?" Come on. Be honest with yourself right now and look truth in the eye.

Does the following list sound familiar to you also?

- You have to pray and read your bible.
- You have to pray at a certain hour of the day.
- Go to Church.
- Invite people to church. (They call that "witnessing.")
- Pay your tithe.
- Go to Sunday school.
- Go to a Christian school.
- Wear certain clothes
- Wear your hair in a certain style.
- Speak in tongues.
- Become a member of a church.
- Do this and do that.

While I don't imply that any of the above is wrong, and neither do I wish for you to think that I don't believe in doing some of them for myself, I have found that this is not the *secret* to finding the door to the presence of my Lord.

Don't despair though. This book is written for people like you and I who finally decided that "*It has to be for real, or else it must not be at all.*"

I do not believe anything on that list even comes close to the issue of how to live the Christian life. I believe that those things become a part of your life after you discover the secret to this deep, wonderful life.

In fact, I believe that this list has one bone-crushing flaw. When you go through it again, (maybe you feel like adding a few of your own to this list, to make it more interesting), you will discover that it assumes that it is possible for us to decide one day, "I am going to live this Christian life."

Numerous seminars and Sunday school lessons have merely added to this long "how to do list," but all it did was make it more and more obvious, that on your own, *you cannot live this Christian life."*

Many persons are religious by the influences under which they come, certain people become good, bad, or indifferent. But when a man lives in the presence of the Lord, he has fixed principles, which rule his heart, and guide his life. He fears God, not because others fear him, but because God is "to be held in reverence of all them that are about him?"[1]

He believes revealed truth, not because others believe it, but because he is sure that the Lord has spoken it, and therefore he knows it to be true. If anybody denies the faith he stands up to it, for it is precious to his heart. His moral conduct and his spiritual life are upright, true, sincere, and reverent; not because of the prejudices of education, or the force of example, but because the Lord has placed within him a new heart and a right spirit.

He does not resort to another man's religious cistern; for there is within him "a well of water springing up into everlasting life"[2] He discerns

---

[1] Ps 89:7.
[2] John 4:14.

33

between truth and error; for he has learned the gospel for himself by the teaching of the Holy Ghost. He follows after holiness because he walks with the God of holiness, and the law of the Lord is written upon the tablets of his heart. The gospel of the Lord Jesus, he receives by the witness of the Spirit. It is true to him, whether others receive it or reject it: he could part with anything and everything sooner than quit his hold upon the everlasting truth of God. This is to be a tree by a well, to have a religion based upon principles, to live by vital contact with the Lord.

We need to tap "the deep that coucheth beneath"[1] If we can reach the secret fountains, and also say to God, "All my fresh springs are in thee," then shall we find nourishment for our branches, and our fruit and leaf will never fail.

"Dwell deep" is a prophetic word of much value to Christians.

To live upon land-drainage and casual rains may suffice for ordinary plants; but the trees of the Lord which bring forth much fruit need to penetrate below the topsoil and reach the secret fountains of grace.[2]

At this point we have to ask ourselves this important question: "How did our Lord manage to live this Christian life?"

Did he live it successfully because he wrote the book? Did he succeed because he was God incarnated in the flesh? Did he have resources we do not know about? The answer is a resounding "NO!"

---

[1] Deut 33:13.
[2] From Spurgeon's Sermons

In fact, Jesus stated publicly that He could not live this Christian life. He made sure that everyone would understand it clearly, when he said of himself he could not do anything.[1]

The answer is plain and simple and right in front of our eyes, as you open the scriptures and find that Jesus had an indwelling Lord. Yes, He was in constant fellowship with His Father. Every work that He did was because His Father was living inside Him.[2]

Remember that this Christian life is not associated with any one doctrine or association or organization.

In fact, this Christian life is not native to our life form. It belongs exclusively to another life form! This life can only be lived in *that other realm*. This is the physical realm. Mere mortals live, dwell and die in this realm, but the *realm of the spiritual*, can only be lived with our Lord, living in us, and that is only possible when you allow Him, full control!

He does not lay down rules and regulations, no! He only expects to be exactly that: LORD OF YOUR LIFE, in every aspect of your being.

Jesus said Himself, "Without the Father, I can do nothing."[3]

Praying is part of this life, going to church is part of this life, studying the Word and meditating it, is part of this life, speaking in tongues is part of this life, but this life does not come as a result of doing these things, these things come as a result of entering this spiritual life.

---

[1] John 5:30
[2] John 14:10
[3] John 8:28-29

Gene Edwards, (a Christian Author) tells this about his grandpa:

"Grandpa was a Louisiana Cajun who loved his Lord boundlessly. He was a total illiterate. But that did not stop Grandpa. He would ceremoniously pick up his Bible and hold it in front of him and stare at it intently for long periods of time. The problem was, he almost always held the Bible upside down! Now that is really illiterate; and, yep, that was my grandpa! And yes, he loved his Lord and spoke of his intimacy with the Lord in a way that few literate Bible scholars or Greek-reading theologians could ever hope to match!"

We live this life only by means of the life of the Father. Divine life alone can live this life.

On our own it is impossible, but when our indwelling Lord has control, this life is imparted to us and this *spiritual life* becomes a reality that you could not find in your quest from one sermon to another, or from one church after another.

Chapter Three

*"Do your worst, I am a Christian, Christ is
my help and supporter, and thus armed I
will never serve your gods nor do I fear
your authority or that of your master, the
Emperor. Commence your torments as
soon as you please, and make use of every
means your malignity can invent, and you
shall find in the end that I am not to be
shaken from my resolution."* [1]

Our Christian heritage

In the United States, like many other countries of
the world, the Church's heritage is rich with abundant
historical treasures, of men and women, who made it their
business to know their God, intimately.

They were never prepared to compromise but
were ready to give account of their faith in the Lord, even
in the face of death.

The Puritans were men whose minds derived a
peculiar character from the daily contemplation of superior
beings and eternal interests. Not content with
acknowledging, in general terms, and overruling

---

[1] Andronicus Roman Empire 303 AD. He was thrown in prison
because he did not deny the Christian faith. He was thrown
before wild animals and finally killed by the sword, but he
remained steadfast to the end.

Providence, they habitually ascribed every event to the will of a great Being, for whose power nothing was too vast, for whose inspection nothing was too minute. To know Him, to serve Him, to enjoy Him, was with them the great end of existence ... they recognized no title to superiority but His favor; and, confident of that favor, they despised all the accomplishments and all the dignities of the world. If they were unacquainted with the works of philosophers and poets, they were deeply read in the oracles of God ... Legions of ministering angels had charge over them. Their palaces were houses not made with hands. On the rich and the eloquent, on nobles and priests, they looked down with contempt. It was for Him that the sun had been darkened, that the rocks had been rent, that the dead had risen, that all nature had shuddered at the sufferings of her expiring God. The intensity of their feelings on one subject makes them tranquil on every other, cleared their minds from every vulgar passion[1]

Now we know that sticks are not by nature arrows; they do not grow so, but they are made so; by nature they are knotty and rugged, but by art they are smooth and handsome.[2]

Beware of running about from this meeting to that, contributing your share to the general blowing up of windbags. Your pulpit preparations are your first business. The honest minister puts an arrow on the string, and the Holy Spirit sends it right home. Reach down one of the Puritans, and thoroughly study the work, and you will find yourself mentally active and full of motion.[3]

Elijah's servant went once, and saw nothing; therefore he was commanded to look seven times. So may

---

[1] McCauley's "Milton."
[2] George Swinnock (1627 – 1673)
[3] Charles Haddon Spurgeon

you look lightly upon the Scripture and see nothing; meditate often upon it, and there you shall see a light like the light of the sun.[1]

You see dear reader; this kind of steadfastness is only possible when this light have finally come on inside your bosom. This is not the light of man, or the light of the church, but it is the light from a realm other than this physical. Once this light is received and the fire of its origin kindled, then nothing can deter such a one from its brilliance or keep them from its warmth.

Charles Haddon Spurgeon

Charles Haddon's Spurgeon's Grandfather was a godly man. He was born in 1776 and became pastor at Stambourne, England in 1810 and retained his post in high honor for fifty-four years, or until his death at eighty-eight. He was always happy in the company of young people … they attached themselves to him with a firmness. He often desired he might speak of Christ on his dying bed, which was granted. He said (in those last moments) the gospel was his only hope; he was on the Eternal Rock, immutable as the throne of God. Those who did witness his departure from earth will never forget his joy and peace, and the glorious prospect he had in heaven.

His grandmother was a worthy string for the minister's bow. "Her piety and useful labors made her a valuable helpmeet to her husband in every good word and work."

One Sunday morning in the eventide of this worthy couple she remarked to her old husband that she did not feel well; would stay home, read her Bible and pray, while

---

[1] Joseph Caryl (1647).

her beloved preached. When the old man came back into the manse at noon, his heart broke to find her sitting in the old arm chair, near the fireplace, with her Bible spread out on her lap, her spectacles across it, her head bowed upon her breast – still in death. And her finger rested upon Job 19:21, "The hand of God hath touched me!"[1]

Charles H. Spurgeon was once preaching when he said: "I felt it was but dry work; but on a sudden, the thought crossed my mind, "why, you are a poor, lost sinner yourself; tell it, tell it as you received it!" Why, then, my eyes began to be fountains of tears; those hearers who had nodded their heads began to brighten up, because they were hearing something which the speaker himself felt, and which they recognized as being true to him if it was not true to them."

I vow to glory alone in Jesus and His cross, and to spend my life in the extension of His cause, in whatsoever way He pleases. I desire to be sincere in this solemn profession, having but one object in view, and that to glorify God. Help me to honor Thee, and live the life of Christ on earth![2]

---

[1] Quoted from "The Shadow of The Broad Brim" by Richard Ellsworth Day.

[2] From the "Little Secret Diary" of Charles H. Spurgeon, entry of may 3, 1850

Saul of Tarsus

" Ananias!"

The voice was clear.   "Yes, Lord," Ananias, answered.

"Go over to Straight Street, to the house of Judas. When you arrive, ask for a man from Tarsus. His name is Saul. He just had a vision in which he saw a man named Ananias come in and lay hands on him so he could see again."

Ananias received the instruction with a shock going through his system.   The name, "Saul of Tarsus," sent waves of fear throughout the entire body of believers inside and outside of Jerusalem.

Only a few weeks ago, this hypocritical Doctor of the law, was standing as prefect, carrying out what he called "Justice", as his followers dealt the death blow to the wonderful brother Stephen.   "Stephen of all people!" the murmur were heard throughout the entire circle of believers.

Many of them could not help but to feel hatred towards this man who was supposed to be one of the spiritual leaders.

"Saul of Tarsus!"   His name would make fear become a reality.   Yes, his name would bring the thoughts of vengeance to your mind.

"But Lord," Ananias exclaimed, "everybody's been talking about this man and the terrible things he's done to the believers in Jerusalem. And now he's shown up here in Damascus with papers from the Chief Priest, authorizing him to arrest every believer in town!"

Without waiting to hear what God had to say, he continued, "surely, you don't mean Saul? The one who just murdered brother Stephen?"

But Jesus said, "Go! I've picked Saul as my personal representative to take my word to the Gentiles, to kings, and to all the people of Israel. I'm about to show him what he must suffer for My name."

Reluctantly at first, Ananias obeyed Jesus and found Saul, just like the Lord said he would.

Looking at this small but intelligent man, Ananias found his spirit strangely touched by the hand of God. His body shook with the presence of the Spirit as he laid his hands upon him and said, "Brother Saul, my name is Ananias. The Lord Jesus, whom you saw on your way here, sent me so you could see again and be filled with the Holy Spirit." Instantly, something like scales fell from Saul's eyes, and he could see again.

Ananias immediately noticed that something was different in this devout man. His eyes radiated a glow and the presence of Almighty God, was visibly present on him.

He got up, was baptized, and then sat down and ate a hearty meal with them. Slowly the atmosphere was changed and it was not long and everyone agreed that something had happened to him.

Saul ended up staying with the believers in Damascus for a few more days. Then he went right to work, preaching, saying, "Jesus really is the Son of God!"

With amazement and shock those who heard him would say, "Isn't this the man who persecuted Jesus' followers so badly in Jerusalem" Didn't he come here to perhaps drag even more Christians off to jail?"

The more Saul preached, his meetings got more powerful. Soon the Jews in Damascus couldn't argue with him or refute his proofs that Jesus was the Messiah.

Not long, and they decided to kill Saul, but he found out about their plot. He escaped from the city by being lowered over the city wall in a large basket.

Back in Jerusalem, Saul tried to join the disciples, but it did not go that easy. Not too many trusted him yet.

Finally, Barnabas, a trusted friend of the others, spoke on his behalf, "The Lord dramatically revealed Himself to this brother Saul on the Damascus road. Since then, Saul has laid his life on the line brethren, boldly preaching in the synagogues in the name of our Lord Jesus. I reckon we need to give God a chance and see if this is real or not." Not long after, the disciples accepted Saul as one of them

He preached boldly in the name of Jesus all over Jerusalem. When the Jews there, attempted to kill him, the other believers got him safely out of town, took him to Caesarea, and then sent him to his hometown of Tarsus.

Shortly after this, Saul adopted the name of Paul, and in the ensuing years would impact the world like none other after him.

Several times, he would escape death. An angry mob in Iconium tried to stone him along with his friend Barnabas, but they were able to escape to Lystra. On another occasion the Jews from Iconium who were chasing Paul and Barnabas were able to turn a murderous mob against them. They stoned Paul and dragged him out of the city, leaving him for dead. The disciples gathered around him and Paul was miraculously able to rise up and walk back into the city. The following morning, him and Barnabus, left for Derby.

Time and again, Paul was caught, and time and again, he escaped. He was thrown into prison in Philippi, but God would send an earthquake and the prison doors were opened. Miraculously, the chains fell off from his ankles and he escaped.

Later, he was imprisoned in Jerusalem, until forty men swore to neither eat nor drink until they saw Paul dead. When the Romans found out, they moved him to Caesarea. There he was in jail for two years and then sent to Rome to be tried before Caesar. On the way, survived a shipwreck only to be bitten by a deadly, poisonous snake. Paul, however, shook the serpent off into the fire and with the gentile group sitting with amazement written on their faces, he used the moment to preach Jesus, and many were saved that day.

Later, when he would write to the Corinthian church, Paul gives a further account of his sufferings: "I have worked harder, been put in jail more often, been whipped times without number and faced death again and again. Five different times the Jews gave me thirty-nine lashes. Three times I was beaten with rods. Once I was stoned. Three times I was shipwrecked. Once I spent a whole night and a day adrift at sea. I have traveled many weary miles. I have faced danger from flooded rivers and from robbers. I have faced danger from my own people, the Jews, as well as from the Gentiles. I have faced danger from men who claim to be Christians, but they are not. I have been hungry and thirsty and have shivered with the cold, but I would have it no other way."

He would clearly state that he discovered there is nothing and no one who can separate him from the love he found in his Lord.

Paul, like so many of us, came to the realization that this life is not in the words of man's wisdom or in mere eloquency of speech. He made sure that his readers understood that there is another realm around us, which the natural man knows nothing about. In fact, Paul said to the Corinthian church, that the natural man is incapable of understanding the things of the Spirit of God.[1]

In the twilight moments of his life, shortly before his execution, he wrote to Timothy, his spiritual son, and said, "For I am already about to be sacrificed [my life is about to be poured out as a drink offering]; the time of my [spirit's] release [from the body] is at hand and I will soon go free. I have fought the good (worthy, honorable, and noble) fight, I have finished the race, and I have kept the faith.[2]

At the age of approximately 64 years of age, this warrior of the faith was beheaded during Nero's reign.

You see, it is men like these who offers you and I enough reason to ask, "Do I know my Lord close enough to walk in the same worthy manner?"

Mere religion will not be enough to carry you through moments like those noted above.

---

[1] 1 Corinthians 2:1-14
[2] 2 Tim 4:6-7 AMP

Terrorists in Rhodesia

The Rhodesian war was experiencing its worst moments. Terrorists have been involved in the worst kind of acts in the country, and it did not seem to get any better.

Every available man was drafted into the war, and even as Pastor of a small church, I was no exception, but had to defend the country like all the rest.

Often times, small country churches were the targets of some of the ungodly, hard-core terrorists.

A pastor of one of those small country churches reported an incident where two terrorist men, boldly walked into the building, where the members were joyfully singing the hymns of the church.

These men were carrying their AK-47 rifles, and noisily entered the peaceful little group of "faithful worshippers," pointing their rifles recklessly into the small audience.

The pastor reported that these men walked to the front of the church, just as the members were singing the last verse of "I'll fly away."

One of the terrorists spoke out aloud and while pointing his rifle at the audience, challenged those who were ready to actually "fly away" to stay put, and those who were not, to make their way out of the little building with haste. Except for the pastor and his wife, only three members remained while the others dashed for the door.

The pastor and his small band took hands and began to pray, knowing fair well that the end has arrived.

Suddenly the terrorist spoke in a more friendly tone, and said, "Well Pastor, now all the traitors are gone, and my friend and I can join you in prayer."

This remarkable incident has stayed with me through the years, knowing that it is not every one who joins in Zion's songs, who have the steel that heaven's relationship affords.

Polycarp

Go with me for a brief visit, back through the pages of time. Hold onto your seat though, because this journey can be rough. This is not a highway of easy remembrance, no, it is the rough old pioneer roads that godly men and women have beaten, with a persistence that still inspire the hungry like you and me.

Do you have your seatbelt on and ready for the visit? Let's go then. Hold on. It might be a little bit of a rough ride...

The kindly, old bishop entered the arena under armed guard. The stands were filled with an angry mob; their shouts filled the air.

Suddenly, a voice from heaven spoke to the Bishop, saying, "Be strong, Polycarp, and play the man." Despite the noise from the crowd, many of those who stood nearby also heard the heavenly voice.

Once inside the arena, the soldiers quickly brought Polycarp before the Roman proconsul. Polycarp, the well-known Bishop of Smyrna, was the last living link with the twelve apostles, as he had studied under John. AS soon as the crowd learned that this famous bishop had been arrested, a great cheer went up.

The proconsul tried to get Polycarp to deny Jesus Christ: "Swear by the fortune of Caesar. Take the oath and I will release you. Curse Christ!!"

The bishop stood firm. "Eighty-six years have I served the Lord Jesus Christ, and He never once wronged me. How can I blaspheme my King who has saved me?"

The proconsul threatened, "I have wild beasts ready, and I will throw you to them if you do not change your mind."

"Let them come, for my purpose is unchangeable, replied Polycarp.

"If the wild beasts don't scare you, then I will burn you with fire," said the proconsul.

"You threaten me with a fire which will burn for an hour and then will go out, but your are ignorant of the fire of the future judgment of God preserved for the everlasting torment of the ungodly. But why do you delay? Bring on the beasts, or the fire, or whatever you choose; you shall not move me to deny Christ, my Lord and Savior."

When the proconsul saw that Polycarp would not recant he sent the herald to proclaim three times in the middle of the stadium, "Polycarp has professed himself a Christian."

As soon as they heard these words, the whole multitude of Gentiles and Jews furiously demanded that he be burned alive. Immediately dry wood was brought out and heaped in the center of the arena for a bonfire.

When they were about to nail him to the stake, Polycarp said, "Leave me as I am; He who gives me strength to endure the fire will enable me to remain still within the fire." They agreed to this and simply tied his hands behind his back with a rope.

In his final prayer, he prayed, *"O Father, I thank You, that You have called me to this day and hour and have counted me worthy to receive my place amongst the number of the holy martyrs. Amen."*

As soon as he uttered the word, "Amen," the officers lit the fire. The flames rose high above his body, but miraculously, he was not burned. Those who watched said, "He was in the midst of the fire, not as burning flesh but as gold and silver refined in a furnace. And we smelled such a sweet aroma as of incense or some other precious spice."

Since the fire did not hurt him, the executioner was ordered to stab him with a sword. As soon as he did, so much blood flowed from the wound that it put out the fire.[1]

Andrew

Yes, indeed, our history is paved with godly people who knew that what they had could not be replaced or removed, with or by, anything that mortal man could devise.

See Andrew, as he boldly looks the governor in the eye. "It is good for you, the judge of men, to first know your Judge who dwells in heaven," he said, his voice ringing with the force of truth. "After you know Him, then worship Him, removing from your mind false gods and blind idols."

Christians all over the empire were being executed in obedience to a decree from the Roman Senate. Peter had been crucified a year earlier, and before this year would end, six more of the original disciples, including Andrew, would be executed. Of the twelve, only John would remain on earth.

Andrew had voluntarily come to face Aegaeas, the governor; to persuade him not to persecute the many Christians; Andrew had brought to the faith in the city of Patras.

Andrew's words angered the king. "Are you the same Andrew who has overthrown the temple of the gods and persuades men to be of that superstitious sect which Rome has now commanded to be abolished?"

---

[1] Foxe's book of Martyrs.

Andrew answered, "The princes of the Romans do not understand the truth. The Son of God, coming from heaven into the world for man's sake, has taught and declared how those idols, whom you so honor as gods, are not gods, but rather cruel devils, enemies to mankind. They teach the people to do things that are so offensive to God that He turns away. In serving the devil, people fall into all kinds of wickedness, and after they die, nothing remains for them but their evil deeds."

"Enough!" the governor commanded. "Do not teach such things anymore or you will be fastened to the cross with all speed."

Andrew answered, "If I were afraid of the death of the cross, I would not have preached about the majesty, honor, and glory of the cross."

The governor then pronounced sentence, "This man is starting a new sect and taking away the religion of the Roman gods. I hereby sentence him to death by crucifixion."

As Andrew was brought toward the place of execution, he saw, from afar off, the cross prepared for him. Instead of the fear that might be expected, fervent love for Jesus rose up in his heart. He cried out:

"O cross, most welcome
and long looked for! With a
willing mind, I joyfully
come to you, being the
disciple of Him who hung
on you."

As he neared the cross he said:

"The nearer I come to
the cross, the nearer I

> come to God; and the
> farther I am from the
> cross, the farther I
> remain from God."

For three days, the apostle hung on the cross. As long as he could move his tongue, he instructed all who stood nearby, encouraging them, "Remain steadfast in the word and doctrine which you have received, instructing one another, that you may dwell with God in eternity, and receive the fruit of His promises."

After three days, the Christians asked the governor to take Andrew down from the cross and release him to them. But Andrew, hearing their plans, cried out, "O lord Jesus Christ! Don't let Your servant, who hangs here on the cross for Your name's sake, be released to dwell again among men! Please receive me, O my Lord, my God! You I have known, You I have loved, to You I cling, You I desire to see, and in You I am what I am."

Having spoken these words, he committed his spirit into the hands of his heavenly Father.[1]

---

[1] DC Talk – "The voice of the martyrs." Published by Bethany House Publishers 1999

Only Divine Revelation

Before being murdered in a gas chamber, a Jewish man inscribed the following words on the wall of a Nazi camp where he had been incarcerated: "My God is there as the sun is still in the heaven above the thick clouds and He will never change though I walk under heavy clouds of unbearable pain and agony."

Religion will only suffice while the day is full of sunshine and the storms of life are beyond the horizon of your own existence. The real test will come when the fire is in your face, or the billows howl and the waves would pull you under.

Christian faith is not an object of science and philosophy because our human knowledge cannot prove the existence of God. God is not subject to time or space as humans.

God was before the creation of all. He has never changed and will never change forever. It is foolish for man to try to judge God by his science and knowledge. Man can know God only by divine revelation of God.

Dr. Yongi Chow tells of an incident where at a Paris crusade many years ago, a professor came in to share his wonderful testimony with him. This man had been an atheist and could not believe in the existence of God. One day a gypsy visited him and shared his testimony about Jesus Christ. The gypsy was not a learned man. He was just living everyday from hand to mouth but his testimony radiated with a confidence, which was something, the professor could not forget.

As they talked the professor asked, "Where is God? How can Jesus Christ be God's Son?"

"I cannot prove it to you, Sir," the gypsy said. "But I know one thing, if you repent of your sins and receive Jesus Christ, be baptized in water and also in the Holy Spirit, you will believe in God's existence."

"But, how can I repent to God for my sins if I don't believe he is/"

"Well, I don't know very well about that," the gypsy said, but anyway if you repent of your sins and receive Jesus, you will be able to believe. Try it!"

After the gypsy left, the professor was troubled a long time and then decided to find out for himself. Kneeling down, he began to talk to God. "God, I do not know if you truly exist or not. But I want to repent of my sins anyway."

Trying his best, he said he recalled one sin after another, asking God to forgive him. "Jesus, if you're truly the Savior and Lord, please come now... come into my heart."

He said, as he opened his heart sincerely before God, he began to realize how much he really needed a Savior and how much he needed his sins to be forgiven. His prayer of repentance changed to deep lamenting and weeping, pounding the floor with earnestness as he prayed. Soon, he recognized his burden had lifted and the presence of Jesus was in the room with him. [1]

God is not revealed to people through an excellent delivery of human logic. He is revealed to seeking people who earnestly seek Him with their whole heart.

---

[1] From: "Born to be Blessed, by David (Paul) Yongi Cho.

Only God Will Do

As we hear about inspired dramas like the ones you just read about, one cannot help but to throw all of pretence to the wind and all of mere religious cliché's into the cesspool of human nonsense in search of reality for self.

You feel like the prophet Elisha when he picked up the mantle of his Mentor, Elijah, crying out from inside his bosom, saying, "where is the God of Elijah?"

It is not good enough to merely sit on the bleachers with the rest of the spectators, and observe or admire the ones who have broken through with God.

To share with the woman at the well, when she finally ran to tell the others, "I have found a man..."

To climb the mountain with Moses, who would ultimately say to God, "Let me see your face!"

To dance with David, in spite of the criticisms of the relatives, because "He has turned my mourning into dancing." Or "I will enter His gates with thanksgiving in my heart," because "In His presence there is fullness of Joy, and at His Right Hand, there are pleasures for ever more."

To cry out with Isaiah, saying "Here I am, send me!"

To be there and share in the announcements of the Mary's who delightfully runs through the streets of their disappointments and say, "Peter, John, Thomas, our Lord is alive. He lives! The stone is rolled away, and our Lord is alive!

As you move out of this place of loneliness and despair, where it seems as if God is no more alive than any of the other gods of the ungodly, you understand the cry of St. Andrew, when he said, "*those idols, whom you so honor as gods, are not gods, but rather cruel devils, enemies to mankind. They teach the people to do things that are so offensive to God that He turns away. In serving the devil, people fall into all kinds of wickedness, and after they die, nothing remains for them but their evil deeds."*

Deep down in your heart, in the deep recesses, where only God's Spirit can dwell, you find yourself seeking. Seeking for something more than just a church service.

You find yourself seeking for more than just a sermon, or a song, or a list from someone's imagination. The search is not mortal, or inspired by self. You know that there must be someone real, someone to share life itself with. Someone to make everything you have ever heard of real and tangible.

You've already decided that the answer is not in anything that man can produce. No, this quest is for a counterpart that is out there somewhere, and you will not settle down until you have found that something or someone.

You know you belong to something more than just an association, or a club, or a society of sorts.

Some of you have tasted it once, for some, just a brief while, only to be swallowed up again in man's pretence world, but now that is not enough anymore.

This is why you are reading this book. You are hungry and thirsty for that which can only be found in the realm of the spirituals, for you know that is where your Lord, your Beloved, will be found.

The song from your heart is shared by many others, who like you, is searching from place to place while you're singing:

*"Many waters cannot
quench love, neither can
floods drown it.
If a man would offer all the
goods of his house for love,
he would be utterly scorned
and despised.
Make haste, my beloved, and
come quickly, like a gazelle
or a young hart [and take me
to our waiting home] upon
the mountains of spices!"*

This search will not be in vain dear Reader, for He is searching also for you, and He will not stop until you are found.

Right at this moment you can almost feel the passion of David when he said exactly what you and I, together with millions of others, feel:

*"Only this one place will do, in the cleft of the Rock, that shadows a dry, thirsty land, From the end of the earth will I cry to You, when my heart is overwhelmed and fainting; lead me to the rock that is higher than I [1]
I spread forth my hands to You; my soul thirsts after You like a thirsty land"*

And also,

*As the deer pants for streams of water,
so I long for you, O God.
I thirst for God, the living God.*

---

[1] Ps 61:2; Ps 143:6

When can I come and stand before him? [1]

Bunyan said, *"Does not your mouth water as you hear this?"* Do you not say, *"Is all this really prepared for me? Then, why do I not have it?" Ah! Why not, why not indeed? In my Master's name, I do assure you that "all things are ready" for all who will seek him, for every soul that will trust him. If ye seek him not, if ye will not believe, there is no mercy for you, but if you seek heartily and trustfully, ye shall assuredly find it, for it was prepared for you long ago by him who has gone to heaven to prepare glory, having already prepared grace for you.*

When storms that threaten our walk with God, come, you must remember that we do not make sailors on dry land, nor veterans in times of peace. Christ's rugged warriors who shall do great exploits for him, must be like the Spartan youths, they must be brought up by a Spartan training, and flogged, and made to bear the yoke in their youth, that afterwards they may be good soldiers of Christ, able to endure hardness and to achieve great victories

Let me remind you of the deep dungeon where there was no water, when the iron entered into your soul.

"Yea, the sparrow hath found an house;" that also means that when she had discovered it, she appropriated it. [2]

---

[1] Ps 42:1-2 NLT

[2] Charles H. Spurgeon

Chapter Four

"All true science begins with wonder, and ends with wonder, and the space between is filled up with admiration. If we turn to Providence, the history of the nations, the history of the church, what centuries of wonders pass before us! It is said that wise men only wonder once, and that is always; fools never wonder, because they are fools. The story of the church is a constellation of miracles."[1]

His Counterpart

A man in New Orleans, stood up in Church some time ago, and shared with the congregation about an experience he had that day, with someone at work who asked the question, "If God was so great, how come He would need to create someone to love Him?"

As if a movie was turned on in my mind, the Spirit quickly gave me a lengthy insight into the answer for that question.

God did not create someone to love Him! In fact, man is incapable of loving at the level where God is. Our love is selfish, jealous and very short lived.

No, God created us so that He could love us, because God is love. Jesus told Nicodemus the Pharisee,

---

[1] Coleridge

59

that God so loved the world that He gave His only begotten son."[1]

Allow me to take you on the journey where the Holy Spirit took me as I sat there in the church, listening to this foolish question that was suggested to this Christian Brother.

Go back with me to a time before time. Go with me to where nothing was yet created, and in the distant past, where only God existed. He was alone.

Our God, who is love, had no one to love. He was alone and even though it is too extended for our mortal minds to comprehend, God stood upon nothing, (because there was nothing for Him to stand upon) and created something from nothing and while the morning stars sang together for joy, He bedecked the heavens with stars.

God stood back and admired His work and said, "It is good," but still there was nothing and no one for Him to love.

Next, He created the Angelic host. Beautiful and glorious were they. Powerful and beautiful, each with great celestial abilities given to them, and even though they each had their assignments to carry out, yet He could not love them. Still God was alone. He was very alone and yet so able to love.

Once again God was at work and now angels gathered on the balconies of heaven to observe the Creator.

His attention was now only paid to the blue gem, our planet, hanging perfect upon nothing, and adorned by the sun, moon and stars.

It took but only a short while to bring the universe into place, but now, for several days, God busied Himself

---

[1] John 3:16

on this tiny planet and meticulously provided life forms for the earth, sea and sky.

Filled with curiosity, angels whispered their comments of admiration, each time when God would fulfill yet another amazing task. Over here swimming creatures, then in the sky, souring with grace and color, another and another. On the earth, species without end.

"Such variety. Such perfection, and each one after their own kind," said one of the angels to the rest of the Celestial host.

Day after day, God would be busy as angels merely observed, and every now and again, gasps of amazements would fill the cosmos when created living being after another would take shape.

"Have you noticed that these living creatures are all made in two's? Each with their own counterpart?" One angel said to another.

"They are so unlike us," observed another angel. We are all single, but these creatures are seemingly made, the one for the other. Always two by two!"

The one being spoken to, merely utters a wondering sigh, but like all the other angels, keeps his eye on this magnificent Creator, as He completes each task with intense detail

"The Creator definitely has a plan, that is for sure," utters the first angel without drawing much of a response from any of the others.

They fully understand that the great wisdom in this great God of all creation, never does anything without a plan, but what is it that He is doing?

All they can do is wonder, because it is not their place to stop Him and ask a question. He is too busy and labors without any rest.

"Every 'thing is so beautiful, but I cannot help but to think that He has not yet achieved His final purpose. All of this is for a single climactic purpose, that is for sure," said Gabriel, the great, powerful, mighty messenger, who is created to stand in the awesome presence of this fiercesome, Holy God.

Much attention and respect is paid, the moment this great celestial creature, utters the first whispering sound without taking his eyes off His Creator, to seemingly lecture the rest of the angelic crowd.

Silence fills the balcony of heaven, as they wait to see if he will come out with any more wisdom about the Creator, but something has now drawn his attention back to God.

"Watch!" Gabriel utters only one word, as he points in the direction of the concentrating Creator. The entire angelic crowd leans forward to see what is being pointed to.

God stooped down low, and scooped a handful of clay into His hand. His creative fingers moves skillfully around the clay and His sharp gaze is fixed with great concentration on His work.

Frowns are upon the brow of every angel, including Gabriel, and even the mighty warrior; Michael, has his eyes fixed on what will now obviously come from the hand of this one and only Holy One.

In the back of this incredible crowd, angels are lifting themselves up on their toes with wings spread open wide to balance themselves as they also ensure a clear vision of what has caused the great silence to settle over this otherwise excited multitude.

"I think the beginning of the climax for creation has started," whispers Gabriel, as the rest of the angels nod their heads and as they briefly allow their glances to once again recognize the authority of the great one.

They know if there is anyone who will know God, it will be Gabriel and Michael, but it is clear that at this important moment of creation, not even they clearly understand the plan of God.

Suddenly, the Creator let His right hand gently extend to the surface of this planet with all the fresh, moist vegetation on it.

Then, the moment that all were waiting for happened. A living creature stepped out of the Hand of God. He was muscular and had a fresh, youthful appearance. As man looked up into the eyes of his Maker, a gentle recognition filled his countenance.

He was humble, yet at the same time, proud in his appearance. He looked full into the eyes of God, something that angels could not do.

In the presence of His holiness, they would use their wings to cover their eyes.

A corporate gasp flashed through the heavens, as angels, including the two mighty ones, would stare at this man.

For just a few moments, angels would take their eyes off the magnificent appearance of Almighty God.

"He...he, looks just like the Creator," exclaimed one of the front angels in total amazement.

"Look at God," said Michael as he stood with his one hand rested on his mighty slaughter weapon and the other one pointing at where God was standing.

As one person, every eye turned to the pointed direction. There was God, as they had never seen Him before. Standing, with love radiating from His countenance.

God's eyes were displaying a satisfaction never before witnessed by created beings. It was almost as if God was smiling. No, it was more than just a smile. There was definite admiration present in His glance, admiration for His creation, His handiwork.

"God has company now," comments the outspoken one with his normal observing tone. "He is not alone anymore. Look at His eyes," the angel says once again, but all eyes already were back on God in any case.

It was obvious that God was happy. Yes, God was very pleased and suddenly, the heavenly host broke out in a celestial chorus,

"Praise God ye heavenly host,
Praise Father, Son and Holy Ghost.
Adore Him; worship Him who reigns above all
Let all creation avail them to His call."

Dancing broke out amongst the angels and laughter could be heard throughout the unseen realms. Even on earth, it seemed as if created life could sense happiness as many of them broke free and entered into a release of joy.

Even the wind carried her own song, as she uttered the words,

O you who dwell in the gardens, your companions have been listening to your voice--now cause your Creator to hear it.[1]

---

[1] Song 8:13

In the time to follow, attention would be drawn to man. Angels appeared fascinated with this God-like creature. "He is so... so ... intelligent"

"Yeah, he is, but I don't think that is the right expression yet. He is more than just intelligent. He is... uh..." says another.

Silence was hanging in the air as this angel clumsily tries to find the correct expression, but no one seems to come up with it until Michael speaks out and offers it to the delight of the rest of the curious crowd. "SOVEREIGN!"

Applause went up for the mighty one, and as they settled down, the first angel carried on with his observation. "Yes, he is indeed sovereign. He is so God-like!" Look at him; God had given him the right of choice.

He can actually choose for himself where he wants to be and what he wants to eat.

Morning after morning, God would come and walk with this beautiful creature. When God would come down into the garden, both of them would have so much to talk about. Man would often have a question and then God would have him sit down somewhere on a pasture, or on a rock, and carefully explain to him the answers.

Neither of them appeared in a hurry at any time. They enjoyed each other's company.

One morning, as God arrived in the garden at His normal time, man was found sitting on a high mountain, overlooking the beauty of another created valley. Eagles were flying high above him, reminding them of their presence with sharp cries.

At other times, man would have responded back with some sound of his own, but this morning he seems so occupied.

"Adam, why is your head hanging so heavy on your chest?" God asked as if He did not already know the answer.

Like always, when God and man come together, angels were once again watching and speculating.

This time however, they were only listening. They too had noticed man restlessly going from here to there. Climbing one mountain after another until he finally settled down out of breath where God found him now.

Slowly man lifted his head, and this time without the normal smile on his face, he asked the question that would ultimately puzzle the angels as well.

"How come I am made alone? How come I don't have a counterpart like all the animals that you created? They are all created two-by-two?"

"Now that is a fair question," commented the verbally active angel. "I have been thinking about that myself."

"Hush, you talk too much," says one of the more superior ones. "Let's listen to God's answer."

"Adam, the reason I made you alone, is because you are like me!" Man looked up at God, and now there was an even bigger frown on his brow.

"Well God, explain that to me please. You gave me the potential to love, but I have no one to love?" Man is sitting there on the rock with his hand clasping his breast. "Something inside here tells me, something is missing. Please help me to understand what it is!"

With an understanding smile, God waits patiently until man becomes quiet once more before he speaks and when He does, it is with a question.

"What do you think you are missing Adam?"

Softly, man starts to slap his chest before he speaks and when he does, the verbally active angel is once again the one to pass a comment in the form of a question.

"What does he mean, something is missing?" No one answers the impulsive angel, as they all await man's next statement.

"My own counterpart, God. That's it; I am in search of my own counterpart. Someone that I can love and protect."

Man's face has suddenly lit up as he speaks and the active angel echoes man's answer. "That's it! That is it. That is what has been missing all along. A counterpart for man."

Michael suddenly speaks up and informs all the angels standing in observation. "I have seen that same expression with God, many times. The expression on man's face is the same as that which I have seen with God through the eons of time, as Gabriel and I stood in His presence. That's it! Man is made so much like God, and man has just now expressed in words what we were not able to do.

A COUNTERPART. God also has no counterpart."

"Well Adam, it seems as if the time has come for me to do something about this matter." And suddenly, God allows man to fall into a deep sleep.

"What now?" is the question that fills almost every tongue amongst the angelic host, as God lovingly starts to work on the side of man as he lay calmly in a deep slumber.

God's Hand slips deep into the side of man and He takes a bloodied section from deep within and then goes to work.

Once again, God's face is a trace of concentration. Even though Angels would like to see what God is doing,

He has His back turned to them and takes no notice about the rousing curiosity.

"It is a prototype," Gabriel informs the angelic host.

"What is?" asks another angel. "What do you mean, 'it is a prototype?" Once again, for this short moment, angels would give Gabriel their undivided attention.

"Well, you must remember, that God does everything with a plan in mind. He does nothing impulsive. He does nothing before giving it much thought. Man is created in His image, in His likeness. Look at man, he is just like God, and so unlike all of us. He was made to be a "little god" himself. He was created in every way just like his Maker. He was also created alone, but so able to love, and now, the time has come, where God is going to fulfill in him, what ultimately will be fulfilled in Himself."

The angel nearest to Gabriel speaks up and his face is one big question mark. It is evident that he speaks on behalf of all the others as they all nod their heads in agreement when he spoke.

"I am now utterly confused Sir," and Gabriel readies himself to try and offer a more sensible explanation of that which has not yet unfolded.

"Look," another angel directs everybody back to the scene where God was busy, before Gabriel had a chance to even start his explanation.

That explanation would have to wait for now as man was about to be woken, but in front of him, was beauty beyond comprehension. Man's counterpart was there, alive! And she had eyes just for him, lying there on the thick, luscious grass.

God finally stood back just far enough to where man could not observe his presence. Once again with a smile fixed to His face, He waited for man to wake up from his sleep.   After just a slight stir, man woke up and suddenly sat up quick, as he noticed this counterpart of his.

At first there appeared to be a slight hesitation, but then admiration took its place. His glance was immediately filled with satisfaction and admiration, and that emotion that was inside him from the beginning could now be vented.

Love and admiration joined with satisfaction as he found in her no spot or blemish. Only satisfaction, and nothing else was evident in his posture when he lifted his head to the heavens, knowing that God was there, watching, observing. "Thank you Father. Thank you, she is perfect and everything I had hoped for. Thank you so much!"

"What a prototype," the same angel picked up his conversation again. She is perfect!"

"No," said Gabriel. She is not yet perfect. She, who would ultimately fulfill the prototype, will be perfect. Look at God right now. He is still alone.

For a short while, He had companionship with man, but where is man now? He only has eyes for his own counterpart. That selfish ambition will now take man into the dark shades of life. He has no thought about his Maker right now. It is only she, and her alone."

****

Four millennial days later, angels are once again together on the balcony of heaven. This time, they have been summoned together by the Creator. Each was too glad to show up. They would not miss this creative scene for anything on this eternal moment.

The scene was set. Calvary was the mountain and the Son of God was ready for the moment.

Just moments before, Gabriel had to hold up his hand and Michael had to utter his great voice in a command, when certain of the warriors tried to rush to the scene in defense of Him that they had learned to love so much. This prince of Peace, the darling of the heavens have just been put through so much abuse, that even now, some of the angels are still fuming at what they are witnessing on this mountain of shame.

"Do you remember what I told you on that mountain in Eden, four millennial days ago?" asks Gabriel, and as soon as he spoke, his voice demanded attention.

This mighty creature has the right to respect, because he, unlike most of them, comes direct out of the presence of Almighty God.

Following his question, that provoked nods of agreement throughout, Gabriel now continues.

"Look at the one on this mountain. Whom does he look like?" Glances are now exchanged as they take another look at the Peacemaker.

"Why, he looks like the Father, does he not?" A corporate noise in agreement to this discovery is uttered until another one comes out with another discovery.

"Wait a minute, he...he looks just like the first Adam."

Gabriel smiles at the intelligent discovery of this last angel and then decides it is time to continue with his education.

"I told you that the first Adam was but a prototype of Him that should come. Have you not noticed how this Second Adam, was also in search of His own Counterpart?

Just like the first one, this Adam will only be satisfied when He will now be given the satisfaction of His own counterpart. She, much more than the first Counterpart, will indeed be perfect. She will be presented blameless, spotless, without wrinkle, and She will be pure."

As if mankind have won a battle against the Creator, the earth shook as this "Second-Man" now lifts His head slowly and utters a loud cry: "It is finished!"

The cry went past mortal ears for just a brief moment, but then the sound continued into the realm of the spirituals.

Suddenly, the Creator steps forward, and just like the first time when the first counterpart was created, He now goes to work.

The Roman soldier have taken his spear and opened up the side of the second Man.

"Is He dead?" asks one of the angels nervously, as the Creator now catches the flow of blood and water from the side of this magnificent Adam.

"No, how can He be? He is God Himself. This will be the moment of moments; this will be the great finale of creation. God will no longer be alone after this.

He is only asleep. Asleep for just these few moments, and if you thought the first counterpart was perfect, wait until you see this one. You will now see beauty like never before."

This time, not from the soil and dust of this earth, but from the eternals, the Creator now collects substance. First, He reaches into the heart of the earth and suddenly, graves that have been forgotten; now pops open and collectively the Creator brings them together in this creative moment.

He then reaches into the temporal and rounds up those who up till now had so little understanding. Those who have stood by the side of this second Adam, but have for a brief moment been overwhelmed with doubt, confusion and fear are now rounded up.

Some He finds at the grave where they came to embalm the body of their Lord, only to find that he is no longer there. Others He finds wandering aimlessly, on their way back to an unexcited life at Emmaus, and others here and there, and together, She is created.

God's own Counterpart! He will no longer be alone. Finally, he has someone who is interested only in Him. The only thing that matters to Her will be to look into His eyes and feel His embrace.

Suddenly, a shout of victory rose amongst this celestial host. "Wow, What a moment. The sound of victory is almost unbearable."

Even in the dark domain of evil, respect is demanded, as even they have to bow their heads in defeat and acknowledgement of their own rebellious ignorance of long ago.

For those who have not noticed the triumphant entry yet, they only had to look into the radiant face of the mighty warrior, Michael, as he stood there with his eyes ablaze with admiration and pride, and his right hand on his mighty sword in an attitude of salute. He, like Gabriel is standing on attention!

Then, the second Adam appeared on the horizon of this spiritual realm. He appears like they had never seen him before.

As if pre-arranged, angels with trumpets announce this royal entry, and as the sounds quite down, Gabriel lifts up a load voice in bold proclamation.

> *"WHO IS this who comes from Edom, with*
> *crimson-stained garments from Bozrah?*
> *This one who is glorious in His apparel,*

striding triumphantly in the greatness of
His might?"
"It is I, [the second Adam] who speaks in
righteousness [proclaiming vindication],
mighty to save!"
"Why is your apparel splashed with red,
and your garments like the one who
treads in the winepress?"
"I have trodden the winepress alone, and
of the peoples there was no one with
me."[1]

Everywhere in the realm of the spirituals silence have fallen. A sudden hush had come over everyone. Angels were covering their faces with their wings.

The silence is broken only when the voice of Michael announces for everyone to see.

"Look," he proclaims loudly, and carefully and very respectfully, one angel after another peeps through the feathers of their wings at Michael, only to see that he is pointing at the Creator. This gives them the liberty to turn their faces towards God and there stood He, like they have never before seen Him.

Always Majestic, and all-powerful, but this time a look of completeness had come into His face. Admiration and love is now radiating from His entire being. He is staring down at something, and instinctively angels would follow the direction of His stare.

And there She is! Snow white and pure is His own Counterpart, and she is only interested in Him! For the first time since all of creation, someone who is not touched

---

[1] Isaiah 63:1-5

or influenced, or persuaded by the temporals have her eyes only on Him.

As if the angels are too afraid to speak up, one of the verbally active ones finally would speak with an abated breath.

"Is She not beautiful? So...so...uhm, different. She is temporal and yet she is completely aware of the Spiritual! In fact, She is not mortal. She is immortal."

Gabriel holds up his hand and the wisdom coming from the presence of God is ready to be shared with this crowd.

"She is indeed what was only a prototype in Eden. This is what creation was all about. She is complete, yet not complete. She is corporate and yet single. She will only be corporately complete in another two millennial days from now, but She is His Counterpart. Meet our Lord's Counterpart! His bride," Gabriel proudly announces.

And there in the Eternals were God, like no one had ever seen Him. His eyes were now only fixed on Her. He had no other thought than just Her.

"Listen as they talk to each other," whispers Gabriel;

"Let him kiss me with the kisses of his mouth!
[She cries.] For your love is better than wine!
The odor of your ointments is fragrant; your
name is like perfume poured out."
"O my love [he said as he saw her], you
remind me of my [favorite] mare.
Your cheeks are comely with ornaments, your
neck with strings of jewels.
We will make for you chains and ornaments of
gold, studded with silver."

She says; "My beloved is to me like a [scent]
bag of myrrh that lies in my bosom, He is to
me a cluster of henna flowers in the vineyards
of Engedi."
"Behold, you are beautiful, my love!" [He
says] "Behold, you are beautiful! You have
doves' eyes."
[She cried] "Behold, you are beautiful, my
beloved, yes, delightful! I am only a little rose
or autumn crocus of the Plain of Sharon, or a
[humble] lily of the valleys" [that grows in
deep and difficult places].
But He replied, "like the lily among thorns, so
are you, my love, among the daughters."
With a sigh birthed deep within Her soul, she
answers, "Oh thank you, for You are like an
apple tree among the trees of the wood, so is
my beloved among the sons Under his shadow
I delight to sit, and his fruit was sweet to my
taste.
He brought me to the banqueting house, and
his banner over me was love" [1]

Softly in the background, Divine music started playing. They played the songs of love. The Creator was in love and although no angel understood the song, the Creator and His bride started singing together. They sang of love, which only they could understand.

This was a love like no other...

---

[1] Quoted and paraphrased from the Song of Solomon.

Chapter Five

"Lives there a man with soul so dead,
Who never to himself hath said,
`This is my own, my native land'?"[1]

Golden Calves

Only, do not settle down around the plains of Dan and worship around a golden calf, which religion can so easily offer to us as a substitute for the real God of heaven.[2] The people of God knew how devastated for them that would turn out once before and now, once again, an evil King would make for them a substitute and call it god.

King Jeroboam earned for himself the name of evil repute - "the son of Nebat, who made Israel to sin." He would let the people understand that, "The thing was from the Lord," - But this setting up of the golden calves, this only too successful attempt to sever the sacred bond that bound the people of the whole land in one common allegiance to the temple and the great invisible King who sat enthroned there, bore a widely different character. This was not "from the Lord." It was wholly evil. "The thing became a sin," and the sin of Jeroboam became the prolific source of sin in Israel through all succeeding generations

---

[1] Author unknown
[2] 1 Kings 12: 28-30

Just like this evil king, still today, society panders to man's idolatrous propensities. The "golden calves" may have been intended as a memorial rather than a representation of the Deity. But they were too suggestive of the base, sensuous worship of Egypt.

The thing that is so hard to understand is that they would actually travel all the way to Dan to go and worship something that was not real. Something dead. Something that could not satisfy their innermost desire, but they did it nevertheless.

In the same way, people are doing it still today. Religion is playing its role in society, and while most protestants have no man-made idols to whom they bow down, dead religion have the masses gripped in a vice-like hold and so many are satisfied to remain bowed down low before it's dead demands.

In the bible you can sense the amazement of even our Lord when, speaking about Israel, He said, *"Be astonished and appalled, O heavens, at this; be shocked and shrivel up with horror, says the Lord [at the behavior of the people].*

For My people have committed two evils: they have forsaken Me, the Fountain of living waters, and they have hewn for themselves cisterns, broken cisterns which cannot hold water." [1]

The search is within and not without. The quest is to find for yourself, the satisfaction of a pure relationship with your Lord who is as real as the air you breathe.

The sweet singer of Israel, King David, says it better than I can express in words myself, when he says, "I have hated them that regard lying vanities." [2]

---

[1] Jer 2:12-13

[2] From Psalm 31

That is, those that trusted in their idol gods, which he calls by this contemptuous name, "lying vanities." David was not very respectful to false religions; he called them vanities and lies, and said, "I have hated them that regard them;"

There is nothing innocent about something or someone that leads you to a bitter fountain, or brings you to a tree that brings forth only rotten fruit.

I have often times been humored when coming to a certain church, finding the pastor frustrated because of perpetual spiritual problems in the church.

While at a closer look, you discover that indeed, Jesus is not their Lord. They merely go through the rituals of a planned program. They hear the word of God, but are incapable of conforming to the list of human proportions.

We are incapable of living this Christian life, unless our Lord lives it through us.

I remember as a young kid, how we use to play church. I would be the preacher, standing on a soapbox, and "my congregation" would sit (at least for a while) in front of me, waiting for their sermon.

Ah, it was fun, but alas, it was not real.

The same is still true today, dear reader. You wonder if perhaps the soapbox got bigger and the "game" lasts longer, and the lie is stretched out further? But the reality of it all is still undeniably present, "God is not there, unless He is allowed to live inside our very bosom!"

Faith is never dumb; true faith is a crying faith. If you have a confidence in God of such a kind that you do not need to pray, get rid of it, for it is of no use to you. It is a false confidence and a mere presumption.

Some time ago, my daughter came to me and said, "Dad, I found a church that you need to come and see."

She explained to me that the presence of God was flowing mighty amongst them.

"I will see if I can get you into the third morning service Dad," she excitedly announced to me. She explained that one almost have to have an invitation to attend, as the church could not hold everyone wanting to come.

It was indeed so. The pastor of this fine group of worshippers, graciously reserved seating for my family and I to attend as guests that morning.

From the outset, I was impressed, for as I entered the building the people were respectfully busy with God in one way or another. Some were reading their bibles, while others were praying either around the altars or merely sitting in their seats with eyes closed, talking to their Lord. The atmosphere was electrified with the expectancy for the supernatural.

I recall the time when God told Moses to go down and tell the people to ready themselves; He was planning to pay them a visit. For the next three days, the people washed their clothes, and readied themselves. There was expectancy in the camp. God was coming to them! And then, when He did, the mountains quaked and angels announced His arrival.

Why are we satisfied with the absence of the supernatural? We are serving the same God of the supernatural, and He is our Lord!

The church was packed out to capacity while people were standing around the walls on the inside.

Young people were asked to come and sit on the carpet in the front of the church to make more room for others, still waiting to come in.

Finally, I noticed the fire-Martials in town, coming to the main entrance and requesting the attending Ushers not to allow one more person into the building.

For the next several minutes, lines of cars were asked to pass on as there was no more room for any more hungry visitors The church had a seating capacity of six hundred and fifty people.

The service started and the only way I can explain it, was that it was a "Worship Experience."

It seemed as if people were unaware of their surroundings and occupied themselves with their Lord.

After the service I had occasion to visit with the humble pastor of this Baptist Church.

"Pastor," I said. "I am a Revivalist, and my heart rejoiced over what I witnessed here this morning. Can you tell me, what is happening here?"

The old servant of God's eyes was ablaze with excitement when he took me by the arm and directed me outside into the parking lot. People were still tarrying around the altars.

Outside, he pointed over into the distance to an old stone building a little away from the main sanctuary.

"Do you see that building?" Without waiting for an answer, this servant of God started telling me about the following incident, which I will not forget.

"We have been in that building for thirty-five years. The same little congregation gathered there for all those years, and the only growth we had, were people migrating from another church to ours, while some from us would go from here to somewhere else."

His eyes filled with tears as he continued. "One morning, almost three years ago, after one morning service, one of our faithful men got up in the back of the church, and I remember how he was shaking with emotion.

He was not arrogant or rebellious. No, he was for real. He stood there with his hand raised in the air waiting for me to recognize him. I had just dismissed my people, but no one was leaving.

As soon as I recognized the old man, he spoke with a voice filled with emotion 'Pastor, why is God not showing up in our Church?'"

Standing in front of me, this pastor was once again obviously experiencing the moment, because he took his handkerchief out and wiped a stream of tears from his cheeks.

That moment in the parking area of that church will be indelibly imprinted in my mind. "Here was reality," I said to myself.

As soon as this friend of our Lord got his composure back, he continued with his account.

"You know, Brother Venter, I almost missed it that morning. I came so close to defending myself. I was ready to extend the lie that I was living. I found myself ready to give him the normal jargon, about the fact that God is present where two or three are gathered together, or to say to him that we don't go by feeling, but only by faith."

I realized that God Himself created the moment, and I could not get myself to commit any longer to what was not real.

"I noticed that the eyes of all the other members were on me, and I know they loved me, but they looked so lost. They looked so helpless. They were all looking up at me with expectancy for the truth," he said with eyes once again filling with tears.

He continued to tell me at that moment, truth overwhelmed him. Something that had been pushed aside in his own heart for so long, was now once again surfacing, and he explained that he had the choice of continuing with a lie or face the truth.

He explained to me that even though he knew God was real, he was tired of trying to convince the same people, why miracles are not really for today anymore.

With the elder member still standing in front of him, the pastor said I found myself answering the man with, "I don't know brother. I just don't know."

He explained to me that the old man answered him back in a tender way. "Should we not find out pastor? Should we not find out what is keeping Him from visiting our church? Will that not be the real answer for the community around us and for our families?"

"A spirit of desperation was upon us," he said. "Many of our families were in severe crisis' with children running in many different directions. Some of them into drugs, others in severe rebellion, financial strain upon many of my families. Two of our families facing terminal diseases and a feeling of hopelessness have come over our little congregation. We needed God, and we needed Him now!"

"Church was no longer dismissed," this honest servant of God, explained to me. "No, instead I found myself sinking down on my knees and my congregation surrounded me. Wailing broke out in our church that morning, and for as long as I remember, this was the first time that we were really seeking to find Him. Not a sign, or a miracle or an answer to a problem. No, we were all praying to find our Lord. We knew that we had to, else we may as well close the doors to our church, and stop play acting this thing."

The pastor explained that for the next following weeks, they put an end to their entire program at the church.

"We would come on Sunday's and Wednesdays and we would not sing or preach. We just felt as if we did not want to merely just sing anymore. We wanted to worship, but to worship, we needed to know that He was occupying His rightful place in our hearts."

"Now, it has changed. You saw what happened in the meeting this morning? What you saw here today is really the way we live now. Word got out into the community and people came to see for themselves, and they would not leave again, because they found the Lord for themselves. Not through anything any of us had to do, or the certain liturgy or the motions of habit. No, they discover for themselves that He wants to be found. Those wayward children have returned and are now serving God with their parents. Divine healing became real in our congregation again."

Praise God, dear Reader, this is what it is all about, is it not? Finding Him and being satisfied with nothing less than the truth.

The Wise Men

In a great way, the account of the wise men from the east, speaks to us. You see, these men knew that the Christ was to be found and they went on a quest to do so.

They would be satisfied with nothing else but to find the real Christ. When they finally saw the star, they rejoiced with exceeding great joy.[1]

It was not enough for them just to hear about the Christ, no, they had to find Him for themselves.

You see the light of the star was taken from them for a time, just as sometimes the delightful presence of God is withdrawn from His people. Then, beloved, you walk by faith alone, and not by sight, as these men did, but oh! When the light comes back again, when, after hearing all the chattering of false priests and scribes, and all the talk of Herod the great one, they see the star again, how glad they are! When God sends to his people clear shinings after rain, the brightness of His presence after a time of gloom, then is it with them as it was with the wise men, "they rejoiced with exceeding great joy"

May God give us that modest, unselfish spirit which lives unto Him, and does not want to walk in the sham light of men's esteem! What matters it, after all, what men think of us? The hypocrite proudly boasts if he wins a little praise from his fellows, but what is it except so much wind? If all men should speak well of us, all that we should gain would be this

The reason you are taking the time to read this book is because you and me, like so many others, want to join in that great hymn of old, "*Oh, happy day, happy day, when Jesus washed my sins away.*" Only to continue into the old verse that says:

---

[1] Matt 2: 1-12

" 'Tis done! the great transaction's done;
I am my Lord's, and he is mine:
He drew me, and I follow'd on,
Charm'd to confess the voice divine.
High heaven, that heard the solemn vow,
That vow renew'd shall daily hear:
Till in life's latest hour I bow,
And bless in death a bond so dear."

There is hope!

If there was no mercy, we could not pray. If there was no grace, we could not stay, but oh, thanks be to God, that there is, and just like the Prodigal, we can say, "I don't need to stay here. I am going back to my Father's House.

The enemy would like to think that his hold on our ignorant state is everlasting, and that whatever reason caused you to stagger or fall, would now remain unending. He is a liar and that is all there is about it.

Who told you that the night would never end in day? Who told you that the sea would ebb out till there should be nothing left but a vast track of mud and sand? Who told you that the winter would proceed from frost to frost, from snow, and ice, and hail, to deeper snow?

Who told you this? You know that day follows night, that a flood comes after ebb, that spring and summer succeed to winter? Hope then! Hope forever! For God never fails.

Don't forget that God loves you in the midst of your trial! Mountains, when in darkness hidden, are as real as in day, and God's love is as true to you now as it was in your brightest moments.

No father chastens always; he hates the rod as much as you do; he only cares to use it for that reason, which should make you willing to receive it, namely, that it works for your lasting good.

You will yet climb Jacob's ladder with the angels, and behold him who sits at the top of it. Your covenant God!

Amidst the splendors of eternity, you will forget the trials of time, or only remember them to bless the God who led you through them, and wrought your lasting good by them.

Come, sing on your bed! Rejoice amidst the flames! Make the wilderness blossom like the rose! Cause the desert to ring with your exulting joys, for your Eternal Lord has His eye set on you, and His love is unchanging.

You also, must understand, and should be able to say to those around you, "God likes me too."

You are not an outcast or a second rate Christian, or even one of the peasants from Heaven. No, He has His eyes on you. He created you to love you. You are His workmanship and even now, as you read this book, these words are designed to get you back into shape again.

Remember, He is the Author and the Finisher of our faith. The thing that He started will be the thing that He will see through till the end.

All through the Scripture records there is revealed a vehement contest between man's sin and God's grace, each of them striving to become more abundant than the other. Sin like a dragon pours forth floods from its mouth, and God's mercy as a shoreless ocean rolls in greater majesty.

Just as Jesus himself going among the sick folk scattered healing here and there, and made the lame man leap as a hart, and the dumb tongue to sing, opened blind eyes, drove out fevers and chased away devils, even so, "it is thy touch, Immanuel, it is thy presence, oh Savior of sinners, that heals us of all our sins."

At Peter's Place

Even though the following scene never did take place, it is something, which a lot of people (think) did.

With his head hanging low and his eyes filled with shame, Peter can hardly look the Master in his eye when he is instructed to appear before the Lord following the denial of his friend.

"I am deeply disappointed in you Peter. I really thought I could trust you of all people. Everything I have invested in you and all the time and trust I put in you, was all thrown to the wind, the moment you denied me as you did. What makes it even harder for me to bear Peter is that you did this in front of a little girl. Your fear was not even founded! How do you ever think you will be able to make a stand for me when real persecution comes?"

All this time, Peter merely hangs his head and wiggles his toes. He wishes that the earth would open up and swallow him in, but the sharp rebuke of the Master would continue still even further.

"Now, I can understand in a certain sense why this happened Peter," and for just one brief moment a little flicker of hope starts to glisten in Peter's faded glance, but not for long, because the Master's sharp rebuke destroyed even that last glimmer of hope.

"You are from a sub-standard creation, Peter. I am from a different realm. I am from the realm of the Spirituals, but your nature is one of sin. You were a born sinner Peter, and you will have to try and live this life by your own efforts. You will have to get together with the rest of the Apostles and draw up a list for yourself, and try your best to live by it. Watch how you dress, talk and behave. Praying at a certain time of day is going to be very important and make sure that you don't try and prosper in anything you do.

I will send people to keep you humble and I will make sure that you remain poor. Prosperity is not good for your soul, and the more you struggle, the better your chances of making it into eternity!"

If for just this one brief moment, lets say that is what Jesus said to Peter, then do you realize what that would mean?

It would mean that we are all second-class Christians, from an inferior tribe of sinful rebels, whose nature it is to sin.

It would mean that there are two ways to live this Christian life; one way for the Lord as the Superior being, and another for us sub-species. Therefore, performance becomes everything. We have to live merely by the outward. The inward means very little.

No, that is not it. That is not how we will live. That is not who we are. Jesus made it very clear that without the indwelling of the Father, he also, could do nothing. Without the indwelling of "His Lord," he also would stagger, falter and fail. [1]

He made it clear in his teaching that the evidence of the Father, living in him, was seen in the works that he did.

To the disciples he said later, in the exact same manner, he also would indwell us. Our Lord, who is so capable of love, so successful in relationship, so eager to please, will indwell us.

This spiritual realm will come and live in us, and we in it!

---

[1] John 5:18-19, 30; 14:10-11

The truth of the matter is this. After Peter's denial problem, the matter was dealt with much different. I think it sounded more like this:

"Mary, run quick. Go to Peter's place and tell Simon, that I am not dead. Tell him there is hope for him, Mary. Tell him not to despair, I am in charge."

As Mary reached Peter at his place of despair and loneliness, his head literally jerked up when she shouted his name, "Peter!"

"Peter, I just come from the grave. It was open and the stone is rolled away. I was still so confused about the whole thing, when suddenly our Lord appeared in front of me, Peter, and He made sure that I understood that I had to get a hold of you, to let you know, He lives! Peter, our Lord is not dead, and He sent you a personal message, not to despair. He loves you Peter, He loves you!"

Later, when Jesus would take time to share personally with Peter, I think that maybe it would have gone something like this: "Did you learn your lesson now friend?" In the eyes of Jesus, there would be no sharp rebuke or flash of anger. A sympathetic smile assured Peter of his Friend's sincere love. "You must never forget Peter, that in yourself, nothing can be accomplished, but after this, I will personally indwell you my dear friend. From here on you will know that everything I did, you also will be able to do, because the Father and I will now come and dwell inside you."

Later, our Lord made it clear to Peter and all the rest, not to even think about going into Jerusalem and the rest of the world without receiving the Holy Ghost.

Then, and then only Peter, will you be able to be successful. Then and then only, will you see the supernatural. Then, will you see the sick healed and prayers answered for real, because I will indwell you.

For so long, churches have claimed this baptism in the Holy Spirit, merely as a one-time experience, instead of a continuous relationship. This should become the beginning of a long lasting relationship that would make an excellent witness out of you.

Someone who can honestly tell the world out there, "I know Him." You know Him not because of a single, one-time encounter, but you know Him because He lives inside of you.

The star of His bright being hovers over your life and those who come in contact with you know that he is your indwelling Lord.

He never meant for us to merely look at this "Upper-Room" experience as merely the "Baptism of the Holy Spirit," where you receive your "tongue" and now you also, have a "diploma" to hang on the walls of your religious heart, saying, "I have it also."

No, it is more than merely tongues; it is your indwelling Lord coming to you with Power beyond mortal comprehension, saying to you, "I will now live this life in you!"

Chapter Six

You are like the primrose by the river's brim,
or the buttercup and the daisy in the field that
is visited with the scythe. That is all we are;
not cedars, not oaks, not rocks, but flowers of
the field.[1]

The Destiny Child

The heart-rending cry of a barren Rachel can still be heard over the hills of man's deceitful past.

The sound of passion reaches the ears of immortality, when she cries to her counterpart, Jacob, saying, "Give me children or else I will die."

Unlike Jacob who found himself so frustrated, unable to speed to her rescue, and answering her with a "Am I God to do something about this?" our Counterpart, our indwelling Lord, can and will do something about it for you.

You see dear friend, every time whenever God showed up, the state of barren-ness was abolished.

Sarah was barren, until that day when the Lord appeared to Abraham by the oaks or terebinths of Mamre, while he sat at the door of his tent in the heat of the day.[2]

The visit of our Lord would change things for the two of them. Her destiny child, Isaac, would be born not

---

[1] Spurgeon
[2] Gen 18:1

long after, and barren-ness would become something of the past.

Once again, a few years later, Isaac would pray much to the Lord for his wife because she was unable to bear children; and the Lord granted his prayer, and Rebekah his wife became pregnant. Her destiny child, Jacob, would be born, because God showed up. [1]

Oh, the joy of finally holding your own, in your hands. The joy of knowing that this is really your very own, and that barren-ness is gone. It is in your past and you no longer have to merely admire others holding the gift of life, folded in their arms.

You also, have your own "destiny child" hidden in your bosom, only to be impregnated by the intimate presence of your own Beloved Counterpart.

But come with me to the third barren one, Rachel. She was one of the daughters of Laban, from Haran. The bible says that she was beautiful, but she was barren.

What a horrible indictment! She was beautiful, but...

We may have everything in place, but...we are barren. She was beautiful, but empty.

We have a good-looking church, but...we are not able to bear life. We have the necessary academical qualifications, but we do bring forth what we are destined for.

Filled with desperation and anguish. She utters a heart-rending cry that still reaches the boundless horizons of today.

"I need a child! I need to be fulfilled!"

What follows after this moment is easily missed, as it is so easy to read it as merely part of history.

2.Gen 25:21

Because of her desperation, this beautiful young lady did something that is so similar to our own situation.

"Bilhah," she cried out. "Come here," she summoned her maid. The maid stood in front of her with hands folded in a humble posture, ready to hear the instruction of her Mistress.

"You understand my situation. I desperately want a child of my own, but I can't. I am barren Bilhah. The only way this matter can be resolved will be like this; tonight, you will sleep with my husband, and I want you to carry his child. You must remember though, that it will never be your child. It is going to be mine. You will only be the vessel that will bring fulfillment for me."

Startled by this instruction the maid shudders, but she knows that a horrible sentence will await her, should she refuse to fulfill her Mistress' command.

The scene moves to nine months later, when Bilhah cries out in travail, ready to give birth to "Rachel's child."

"No, it is not going to be done in the normal manner Bilhah. I want you to sit on my lap, and when the baby comes, you will push when I tell you to. You also won't have to worry about the baby, because when he comes, I will have my arms waiting underneath, between my legs. The baby will drop through your lap and then mine. I will be catching the baby Bilhah."

With the last cry of utter travail, the little baby moves from the womb, and into the waiting hands of the non-biological mother, who receives it, with artificial joy.

"Ah, a little boy. God has given me a little boy. I will now name him Dan, for God has vindicated me.[1]

---

[1] Gen 30:6

When Jacob received the boy, the pretence game had to continue. "Thank you Jacob," the excited Rachel would exclaim. You have now fulfilled my life. We now have something in common, you and me."

A year later, this scene would be repeated again, and this time she would cry out, "With mighty wrestlings [in prayer to God] I have struggled with my sister and have prevailed," so she named him Naphtali [struggled].

The sad thing was that she was still as barren as could be. The children, although claimed by her, were not really hers. She named them, but she did not give birth to them herself. It was all one big bluff. It was all a big pretence.

The destiny child Joseph would come, but only after God would change things for her, and only He could change it.

How many times have I seen churches commit this same, shameful act? They would be so passionate for revival, or for the real move of God, but they fail to deal with barrenness in their lives. It is so easy to go to someone else's church, copy what they have received and import it to your own situation.

It is so easy to merely go through the motion, and then call it "yours."

The sad thing is this; they end up being merely echo's of someone else's voice, but the destiny child of God's promise never becomes their own, unless they allow God to remove this hollow feeling from them and subsequently impregnate them with His life.

The truth of her awful disposition would ultimately lead her back to God, and the bible says, "Then God remembered Rachel and answered her pleading and made it possible for her to have children. [Now for the first time] she became pregnant and bore a son; and she said, God has taken away my reproach, disgrace, and humiliation, and she called his name Joseph."[1]

Never was there such joy, as when a Mother hugs her infant to her bosom, saying, "he's mine, all mine," and in her heart she knows this to be true.

Oh, that God would give for you to become overwhelmed with the passionate desire to be filled inside with only that, which is real.

I was greatly pleased some time ago to read about a gentleman telling the account, about a man who had tried to preach another doctrine. He said, "A certain neighborhood, which he spoke of was so impregnated with what was called "the gospel" that he could not succeed with his speculations. He said that if men once drank this gospel doctrine it made them so bigoted in their love for it that the cleverest person could not get them out of it. I thought to myself," This witness is true. An enemy declared it, and it was therefore all the more striking. The subtlest deceivers may try as long as they please, but when we have once fed upon Christ they cannot get us off from him. They call us away from him; they proffer us all manner of novelties; but in vain: "Try our thought! Try our science! Try our purgatory! Try our larger hope!" But we hear the pails rattle, and we hear the swine clamoring, and we are not anxious to taste the mixture, or unite in the festival. We are not so selfish as to steal this new wash from those whom it delights. Let those have it that can feed on it; but as for us, we mean to feed on the bread of heaven."

Should all the forms that men devise
Assault my soul with treacherous art;
I'd call them vanity and lies,

---

[1] Gen 30:22-24

And bind the gospel to my heart.

Hand over Control

A sincere preacher approached me the other day, asking what he should do in order to receive a greater anointing from God.

Before I could answer, he offered his own answer in the form of a question: "Should I pray more, or study more on the word of God?"

This unfortunately is the prevailing concept amongst so many sincere believers who are so aware of their inability to hear our Lord speak to them.

"What more should or can I do?" is the question on the lips of many.

As mentioned earlier in this book, the answer is plain and simple. Nothing we do can *earn* us the right to get more of Him.

Should we pray more, and the answer is a roaring "NO!" Should we study more and the answer once again is a resounding "NO!"

When He touches our lives, then you find that you *WANT* to do more. You desire to be in His presence more, or you want to get to know Him better.

You don't earn it though. Everything you do to earn is like catching someone else's baby between your own spiritual legs like Rachel did. It doesn't work that way. It only works when our Lord decides to bring this spiritual realm into your bosom and your own destiny child is birthed in your own right, and you can sing like the pioneers of old, *"it's mine, it's mine, it's Pentecostal power, and I know it is mine!"*

The golden key is control, control and control. The eternal God wants complete control. He wants to share His glory with no one else. He is a jealous God, and He wants all of you. He does not want you to look at Him, merely as a convenience or as just a "Sunday god."

When seeking this relationship, it takes a serious commitment and you must understand, that our Lord will share His love with no other in our lives.

See what James has to say about this matter to the people of his time, when he says, "You [are like] unfaithful wives [having illicit love affairs with the world and breaking your marriage vow to God]! Do you not know that being the world's friend is being God's enemy? So whoever chooses to be a friend of the world takes his stand as an enemy of God. Or do you suppose that the Scripture is speaking to no purpose that says, The Spirit Whom He has caused to dwell in us yearns over us and He yearns for the Spirit [to be welcome] with a jealous love?" [1]

He does not want you to merely talk to Him in time of trouble. He created you to be His counterpart. He created you out of Himself, and now He wants to live inside you. There is no way, that He will do so, unless you relinquish control and hand it all over to Him.

His eternal plan is not for you to merely become acquainted with Him, or to become part of an elite society of bluffers. His plan is made clear when He says, "And I will betroth you to Me forever; yes, I will betroth you to Me in righteousness and justice, in steadfast love, and in mercy, and you shall know (*recognize, be acquainted with, appreciate, give heed to, and cherish*) the Lord. [2]

Paul was very clear on this teaching throughout his writings. To the Christians at Ephesus he would say, AND YOU [He made alive], when you were dead (slain) by [your] trespasses and sins. In which at one time you walked [*habitually*]. You were following the course and fashion of

---

[1] James 4:4-5
[2] Hos 2:19-20

this world [*were under the sway of the tendency of this present age*], following the prince of the power of the air. [You were *obedient to and under the control* of] the [*demon*] spirit that still constantly works in the sons of disobedience [*the careless, the rebellious, and the unbelieving, who go against the purposes of God*].

Among these we as well as you once lived and conducted ourselves in the passions of our flesh [our behavior governed by our corrupt and sensual nature], *obeying* the impulses of the flesh and the thoughts of the mind [our cravings *dictated by our senses* and our dark imaginings].[1]

The words, "habitually", "obedience" and "dictated" appears throughout.

To the Romans he teaches, "All who are led (*Directed, or Controlled*)[2] by the Spirit of God are sons of God."[3]

Then, two verses further down he says, "The Spirit Himself bears witness with our spirits that we are children of God."

Now, take a careful look at this situation again. While controlled and dictated by the spirits of satan, we "were dead" in the trespasses of our sins.

No matter how long your list is, and no matter how much you try and do yourself, it is not going to take you anywhere. You are not going to break into His glory until our Lord gets control.

"All those," who are led (directed and controlled) by the Spirit of our Lord, are sons of God. Right there and then, you receive a witness from His own person, that you are a child of God.

---

[1] Eph 2:1-3
[2] Italics added
[3] Rom. 8:14

He impregnates you, and giving life becomes automatic. Worship becomes natural and now you become aware of the spiritual realm.

When a man has eaten all he can eat, you may set whatever you like before him, but he has no appetite for it. "*Enough is as good as a feast*," we say.

When a man is forgiven by God, and knows that he is saved, the joy of the Lord enters his soul, and he says, "You may take all other joys, and do what you like with them. I have my God, my Savior, and I want no more."

Ambition ceases, lust is quiet, covetousness is dead, and desires, that once roamed abroad, now stay at home.

This person says, "My God, you are enough for me; what more can I require? Since you said to me, 'I love you,' and my heart has responded, 'My God, I love you, too,' I have more true wealth at my disposal than if I had all the gold mines of South Africa under my control."

People are brought under the impression that they can almost live how they wish and God is still inside of them.

We do understand that God is all over at the same time. It is not even necessary for the writer to expound on this matter, because the Omni-presence of God is a fact, accepted by the church as a whole.

However, I am not talking about the Omni presence of our God. No! I am talking about the indwelling presence of God that brings you into a world that is invisible for mortal man. No eye can see, no ear can hear and the human heart cannot even conceive it.

You must get to the place where you are no longer satisfied to have someone else carry the child, and you lay the charge to it through artificial means. No, like Rachel, you have to get to a place where you say, "It has to be mine."

You and I can pretend as much as we like, but at the end of the day, the fact remain standing. We may excel in the natural, but in the spiritual we are midgets who dwell in the land of giants.

The Salvation Concept.

The weary traveler, with his head hanging low, badly abused by a lying, conniving thief and robber suddenly meets the man from Galilee.

Chains of sin kept him tied to this hateful companion, and no matter how he tried to get free in the past, he still remains a slave under this ruthless taskmaster, called satan.

Now, for the first time,

When Christian walked into church the first time, or wherever he came in contact with the gospel, he came face to face with the beauty of our Lord, and immediately it was love at first sight.

He knew right away that he no longer wanted to remain in fellowship with the enemy. This slave driver, this father of all lies, this robber and thief.

Christian fell headlong in love with the Savior and decides then and there, that this is the life he desires for himself.

Behind the scene much was at work before this moment, that Christian was totally unaware of.

The Holy Spirit has been working in his life, without his knowledge. The prayers of parents or caring friends were all part of the entire scene. A word or a phrase, here and there caught his attention, but in his own eyes, Christian was just one more ordinary person; with his share of weakness. Now, in the face of the Peacemaker, he finally decides, "I want this life for myself."

He finds himself standing at the edge of Calvary's ebb, and one plunge will take him beneath that crimson flow.

The manifold promises of God become a bridge where he can cross over to the other side. "If you accept me, I will give you the authority, or the privilege to become my child."[1]

Earlier on, God's word would ring out in the arena of man's moral defeat, and He announces to each and everyone who will come; *"To them I will give in My house and within My walls a memorial and a name better [and more enduring] than sons and daughters; I will give them an everlasting name that will not be cut off. Also the foreigners who join themselves to the Lord to minister to Him and to love the name of the Lord and to be His servants."[2]*

At Calvary's foot, Christian now bows down and in his heart there is no question any longer that this is where he belongs. This is the reason he was born, and nothing else matter.

On the balcony of heaven a discussion breaks out again as one of the younger angels, hungry to be taught, speaks to one who have witnessed this scene before.

"What will happen to him now? Look at his condition! He is filthy and so abused. This wondering soul, wants to come to God, and just look at him, do you think he has any chance at all?"

The other angel responds smilingly, and says, "Today, you will witness the miracle of the Masters creation.

While Christian bows himself down in humble confession, suddenly the scene of two thousand years ago plays off again as if it had just happened.

---

[1] John 1:12
[2] Isa 56:5-6

"Look, the young angel speaks. The soldier… he has a spear in his hand. Is he…is he… He's going to push that thing up the side of the Master's side?"

With a reassuring gesture of his hand and his face glowing with adoration, the second angel motions the first one to be silent and watch.

As blood and water flows from the side of our Lord, creation repeats itself and suddenly, a transformation takes place right in front of their angelic eyes.

Christian is no longer in the land of the mortals. He is suddenly transformed into the spiritual and enfolded in the Hands of the Creator. For a brief moment, Christian becomes mere clay. Dust as if scooped up from the earth for the first time.

"Look," says the second angel to the younger, in an educating tone. "Look what is going to take place now."

For a brief moment, Christian disappears out of sight as he is taken into the mighty Creator's hand, but then a shout breaks out amongst the celestial host as the Creator transports Christian back to his place of confession.

"Christian is no longer in shame. Look at him…or is it a she… uhm… well I am confused, but one thing is for certain, look at the brightness of this new creature. Please, someone explain this to me," says the young one.

"You have just now witnessed the creation of His Counterpart," says the stronger one with admiration for his Creator, in his voice.

"Now, please explain something to me. What is that chain still around the ankle of this new creature?" as the young one points at this sparkling white creature that suddenly have a glow all around him.

"That is relationship. He is still tied to mortality by birth." Without waiting for an interruption from the first angel, the stronger one continues.

"You see, it works like this; Up till now, he was behaving as a sort of counterpart to the evil one. Legally, man is tied with chains of legislation to the evil one."

"You mean, like one who is kind of married to another?" [1]

"Exactly," answers the stronger one."

Christian is now struggling to get free from the chain, as he desperately tugs and pulls, but to no avail. There seem to be no way that the chain can be loosed, even though his defiled condition no longer exists.

"But, I thought that the Creator have now claimed Christian as His own Counterpart?" asks the young one once again, impatience almost getting the better of him.

"Patience, my young friend. Patience. You will now see the complete plan of Him who knows all things. You see, before Christian can be claimed fully by Him, this relationship have to be destroyed, and to do this, one of the two in this relationship have to die first? Only death can separate the two from one another and only death can break the hold of the chain that now keeps him from climbing the steps to perfection in Him."

---

[1] St. Paul writes: **Rom 7:1-3**

DO YOU not know, brethren--for I am speaking to men who are acquainted with the Law--that legal claims have power over a person only for as long as he is alive?

For [instance] a married woman is bound by law to her husband as long as he lives; but if her husband dies, she is loosed and discharged from the law concerning her husband.

Accordingly, she will be held an adulteress if she unites herself to another man while her husband lives. But if her husband dies, the marriage law no longer is binding on her [she is free from that law]; and if she unites herself to another man, she is not an adulteress. AMP

With confusion now written over the face of the young one, he asks persistently; "you mean, the Creator is going to kill the evil one?"

Laughter breaks out even amongst the other angels who have been observing this scene and enjoying the lesson offered to the young one.

"Not yet, my young friend. Not yet, even though his time is appointed for destruction, but Creator's dealing is not with the evil one. His work is with His counterpart.

"You mean, He is about to kill his counterpart? The one who has just been transformed?" His voice was now trembling with emotional strain.

Before the stronger one could even answer, their attention is drawn back to the realm of the mortals. Christian is led by the hand and then taken only a short distance to an awaiting water grave.

Just as the young one is about to ask another question, the stronger one, puts his finger to his lips, motioning for him to be quiet and watch. Suspense fills the glance of the young angel, as him and others observe the next scene.

Without any struggle, Christian is lowered slowly into the water grave. With eyes closed and peace written all over his expression, he allows the water to cover his entire body, and then suddenly, several things happened at the same time. Silence had now fallen over the entire crowd, on the balconies of the immortals.

As the water covers Christian, suddenly another transformation takes place. For just a brief moment, he totally disappears.

"Christian is now dead!" A strong angel proclaims with such a loud voice, that the young angel almost falls over backwards. This strong angel appeared out of nowhere. His proclamation is made in a legal manner, so that the entire heavenly host could take notice of this announcement.

"The official relationship between Christian and the evil one is now destroyed. When he now comes forth, he will be free from that relationship."[1]

Suddenly, the waters open up and Christian wakes up. It is obvious that he is totally new.

The silence is once again broken with the young one asking, "Was it the grave that made him appear so new?"

"No, my young friend, he was already new at Calvary. Don't you remember, what happened? The Creator did a complete work then, but this is part of his plan to free Christian so that He now can claim that relationship for Himself.[2]

"You mean, up till now, He could not make this claim?" The young one appears nervous.

"Exactly, because up till now, Christian had someone else lay a legal claim to him, that is the reason for that chain."

"Look, Christian is rising up from the grave. Notice his ankles." Another angel interrupts the lesson.

The next moment, Christian sets foot outside the water grave. He is still as white as snow, but the difference now, is that the chain is gone. He no longer has the chain of sinful relationship.

A joyful song breaks forth in the heavenly realm when all of a sudden the Creator Himself, now appears, and stretches His hand out to Christian. In a soft, gentle voice, the beloved One, speaks with the voice of peace. His voice is filled with emotion and tenderness.

---

[1] Rom. 6:4
[2] Rom. 8:16

"Behold, you are beautiful, my love! Behold, you are beautiful! You have doves' eyes. Like the lily among thorns, so are you, my love, among the daughters.
HOW FAIR you are, my love, how very fair! How beautiful is your love my [promised] bride! How much better is your love than wine! And the fragrance of your ointments than all spices!"[1]

His counterpart is ready to walk in intimacy with Him. All that now need to happen is for Christian to walk worthy and to make sure that this relationship remains intact.

As long as he walks this way, the realm of the spirituals will be visible for him...

---

[1] Song of Solomon.

Problems in this mortal realm

Dear Reader, you must keep in mind that just as we cannot pour more water into a cup that is already full, God cannot pour his heavenly blessing into our hearts if our hearts are filled with things of the world. Our hearts must be empty and we must feel our need, in order to receive heavenly blessings.

Humanism

Today, people's hearts are filled with humanism. Passing through the age of the Renaissance, enlightenment and modern day's science and materialism, man has been struggling to build a culture and a world that is human centered. As a result, he does not recognize God but depends on his human efforts alone to accomplish his goals in life.

When people strive to live by their own human abilities only, the kingdom of God cannot come to them. Man is a noble being; yet, if he does not understand he is like the beasts that perish.

Alone, man is a hopeless creature. Without God, he will eventually experience the despair of a sense of guilt and condemnation, being crushed by a sense of nothingness, fear of death and eternal emptiness.

It is not long, and man has to give up entirely, some putting their hand to their own lives, or else settling for something that is created to flirt with man's crazy ideas and fancies.

The world out there is filled with many, who desire fervently to make contact with God, but they have finally reached the place where they have about made up their mind that God is nothing more than a Santa or a Tooth fairy. They have made up their minds that it is not worth their time.

Yesterday, while shopping in Korea, I allowed a tailor to take my measurements for a few suits. The man was a kindhearted individual and understood enough English to where I tried to share the Gospel message with him.

He listened intently at me, but after a while he told me that most all of his family have converted to Christianity, but he continued to tell me about the many struggles within those churches. He told me he had tried everything they said, but he finally made up his mind that nothing was as they told him.

"I tried to find God in those places", he said, "but I found it to be one big lie." The man was genuine and not trying to be malicious. He, like so many millions of others of our time, have about decided that this wild circus which they call "The Church", is not worth wasting their time on.

How sad! How true though. In so many churches, secular humanism have infiltrated the ranks of the so-called Christians, to the point where it is all man's doing and God is merely standing on the outskirts of our memories.

Are we desperate? Sure, most people are, but are they willing to allow the Master a free reign in their lives, to the point of bringing you to the point of death so that life can start?

If you have reached this point in this book, I am convinced that you are at the same place as many others, who have joined with many others, who refuse to remain mediocre. People, who like you and me, will stand on the banks of the river and demand for the presence of God to reveal itself to us, like an Elijah of old.

We will not go away. We will not be silent anymore. We will not allow others to "have the pleasure of impregnation, and we will merely continue to fake spiritual pregnancy. We will not leave empty handed. No, our spirits demand for more, and we know that God is alive, and because He is, we will not settle for anything less.

Pride

Besides humanism, the human heart is filled with pride. Pride is self-satisfaction, an overly generous estimation of one's personal value. The proud child challenges his parents; a proud citizen rebels against his society and nation. As a person becomes haughty he thinks of himself very highly and begins to slight the authority over him and always runs into self-destruction in the end.

Pride is a sure short cut to destruction. If one fills his heart with the dregs of pride, he can never receive heavenly blessings.

Show me a man or a woman of God, and I show you humility. Show me a child of God and I show you love and a sincere heart. Show me a child of God and I will show you one who genuinely cares for his fellow brother.

You see God and God alone, is the one that directs us to the path into this realm of the spirituals.

Show me pride, or arrogance or a person with a high minded and haughty attitude, and I will show you someone who is a supreme bluffer.

I don't care how much you have achieved in life, or how big the church is that you pastor, if you display any of the above characteristics or even any of the lists as mentioned by Paul, [1]then I will show you someone who in spite of their refute, is someone with a lack of the supernatural. They are someone who merely expects their followers to be conformed to the varied lists of humanism.

Listen to what Paul says to the Romans: *"... they became futile and godless in their thinking [with vain imaginings, foolish reasoning, and stupid speculations] and their senseless minds were darkened. Claiming to be wise, they became fools [professing to be smart, they made simpletons of themselves]. And by them the glory and majesty and excellence of the immortal God were exchanged for and represented by images, resembling mortal man and birds and beasts and reptiles."* (Amplified)

As you read this book, the intention is not to persuade you doctrinally in any way shape or form. Neither should you interpret this as an academical wonder (Because it is not), but instead, it is to create in you the awareness, that it is senseless to walk and remain in a world of self, when so much more is available.

There is nothing in ourselves that can satisfy the cry of the human spirit, and if you want to be used by Him, remember that we are all His workmanship, created unto good works.

Every time you run into someone who's quest is the same as yours, remember, the chance are real good, that our Lord wants to use you to shape another in some way. Pride will not allow you that and when pride is present, our Lord is not.

---

[1] Gal. 5:19-21 and Romans 1:21-24

Worldly Things

Not only are humanism and pride hindrances for God's blessings, but also when one's heart is full of worldly things, the kingdom of God cannot come within him either. Those who filled their lives with fornication, licentiousness and pleasure seeking, a hunger for power and money that shines outwardly cannot receive heavenly blessings.

"For all that is in the world, the lust of the flesh, and the lust of the eyes, and the pride of life, is not of the Father, but is of the world. And the world passes away, and the lusts thereof; but he that do the will of God abides forever.[1]

When we cleanse our hearts and turn away from humanism, allow our pride to be broken by God and remove the

---

b[1] 1 John 2:16-27

Chapter Seven

"These things have I written unto you that believe on the name of the Son of God; that ye may know that ye have eternal life, and that ye may believe on the name of the Son of God."-1 John 5:13.

Benefits inside this realm

This book will not be complete unless I add this final chapter.

Once you decide, *"you have had enough of not enough,"*[1] then you are ready to move into the realm of the Supernatural. It does not mean you are moving into perfection, but it certainly means that you realize, your talents, your education and your mortal gifts (if you have any) is not sufficient, to make you eligible to work with the people of God. Neither are you eligible to become know "as a friend of God."[2]

Everyone is born with a unique and different nature. As off springs of Adam, we were born as slaves to corruption and greed. The foundation of our personal nature consists of hatred, anger, jealousy, envy, fear, anxiety, despair, despondency and a deep guilt complex. However, when the grace of God drew us to Jesus, and we were born again, we received a new nature

---

[1] A popular line used by a good friend of mine, Pastor Cleddie Keith, of Florence, KY.
[2] John 15:14-15

and an insight into a realm, which never existed for us before.

Peace

Today, every nation is striving for peace according to its own terms but there is no peace anywhere in the world. Politically, nationally and socially, fear prevails in the hearts of men.

News today, is not popular unless it speaks of evil, murder or deceit. Sickness is multiplying like flies and the crime rate is skyrocketing in just about every place on the face of the earth.

Hospitals are filled with patience whose main problem is of psychosomatic natures and heart attacks are killing untold millions of people.

It is not merely on the outside that man observes many reasons to fear, but on the inside, man is carrying an anxiety that results in numerous other problems.

Anger is overwhelming people in this atmosphere of unrest and trouble and families are breaking apart faster than you can get them together.

There was once an old man who lived like a king, but was insecure and fearful all the time. To find peace, he decided to purchase a painting that would represent peace and tranquility. He offered a huge amount of money to famous painters to prepare something very special on their canvass that would depict the peace he needed to feel. One by one, the painters chose their ideas of peace and painted it on canvas and at last the exhibition day arrived.

The wealthy man entered the gallery and took his time viewing each painting and meditating on the scenes. Some pictures were scenes of a very rustic peaceful pasture with a quiet pond and clouds hanging in the sky. But he passed by those. Another painting showed a farm with a cute puppy dozing on one side with misty figs hanging over a distant mountain slope. He didn't even stop to view that one but passed by quickly. One by one he glanced at the scenes. But his eyes caught the scene of a turbulent waterfall rushing madly down a cliff. On the side of the cliff was a tiny cove. A closer look revealed a very small robin sitting in the cove on her nest of eggs. The expression of the robin was one of rest, peace and serenity in spite of the waterfall. Immediately the rich man knew this was the picture that would bring him peace of mind. As he made his decision, the people around him asked, " Why did you choose that one?"

He said, "In the world today, there is no peace, yet this robin, in her most perilous circumstance found safety in a tiny cove, in spite of the violent waterfall. This picture tells me a peace must come from within, not from without." [1]

Inner peace is something that is obtained only when we become partakers of the Divine Nature of God.

Joy

It is evident that whenever people of the bible came to God, or God came to them, that a feast or at least a great meal were prepared. He who comes to God's table with a good appetite shall never go away unsatisfied. It is want of desire, which often hinders us from spiritual delight; but when the desire is set upon God, it shall be satisfied.

I fear that we often come to the wells of salvation, and yet get nothing, because merely coming to the wells is

---

[1] From: "Born to be blessed, by Dr. David (Paul) Yongi Cho.

nothing. We read in Isaiah, "With joy shall ye draw water out of the wells of salvation."[1]

It is not the wells, but the water out of them, which will refresh the weary one. Do not be content with being here, in your pew, or just to be in church, but long after the living God himself, for He alone can refresh and revive your soul and spirit.

Whenever the religious talk about joy, they merely refer to it almost like a cliché, but it is a well, which will flow from your innermost being.

It is often times referred to as "the new wine", and it has the same intoxicating effect as in the natural. It brings exuberance and emotional relief like none other.

When it happens to you, it is like a spring, breaking open in the desert and while it can be subdued like any one of the other blessings of God, the Child of God will not allow it to be suppressed.

It is a joy unspeakable and full of Glory and the half has never yet been told.

Churches, who do not understand the flow of this "River of God", have been fighting it, like early churches have been fighting any of the other gifts of the Holy Spirit through the years.

They have hailed this fresh outpouring of the Holy Spirit as either a manifestation of demons, or merely an emotional outburst of sorts, but how wrong the religious order have been through the years.

Was it not the religious who crucified our Lord? Was it not the religious who sat in his meetings, merely trying to see how they could trap the Master at his words? Was it not the religious that was so quick to pick up the first stone, failing to see the problem in their own lives?

---

[1] Isa 12:3

Joy is emotion in action.   Show me joy without emotion. God did not make us to be mere zombies.

In fact listen to the words of Paul in the Amplified bible, when he says, *"And my language and my message were not set forth in persuasive (enticing and plausible) words of wisdom, but they were in demonstration of the [Holy] Spirit and power [a proof by the Spirit and power of God, operating on me* **and stirring in the minds of my hearers the most holy emotions** *and thus persuading them], So that your faith might not rest in the wisdom of men (human philosophy), but in the power of God.*

What makes us think that the answer lies in the preaching of a good sermon, or the philosophies of men?

If the answer was in our hands or in the hand of mere Theologians, how come this world is in the mess that we find ourselves in? The answer is still only in one thing, and that is the manifestation of the Holy Spirit, allowing Him to prepare for us the table in the manner that He deems fit.

I have had my share of only meetings, and sermons. I have dropped my bucket like the woman at the well, and I am just too glad to become a witness of the great power of Almighty God in action.

Joy is not just a happy feeling, a worm, happy feeling you're supposed to have now and then when things are going well. It's much more than that. Joy is one of the most powerful spiritual forces in the world.

In the book Nehemiah, he says, "the joy of the Lord is your strength."

If you were to diagram that scripture and remove the phrase, "of the Lord," you'd find what it's truly saying is this: Joy is strength. The two are interchangeable.

That's what makes Joy so crucial. You can't live a life of faith without being strong in the Lord – and when God wants to make you strong; He uses Joy to do the job.

Joy is not just a state of mind. Joy is a very real force, and the devil doesn't have anything that can stand up against it.

We are His workmanship, let Him decide how He wants to shape or change those of us who will ultimately become His perfect bride.

Depression and a spirit of heaviness have overcome believers. Sicknesses like diabetes, ulcers, heart conditions and many others, are all fear and stress related and they are accepted amongst us as if normal and yet they have taken on epidemic proportions.

Nehemiah's advice to the very oppressed people of his time was this; "be not grieved and depressed, for the joy of the Lord is your strength and stronghold."[1]

Joy normally follows true repentance. Have you ever seen clearer shining than that which follows a shower? Then the sun transforms the raindrops into gems, the flowers look up with fresher smiles and faces glittering from their refreshing bath, and the birds from among the dripping branches sing with notes more rapturous, because they have paused awhile.

In his famous poem, King David makes the famous statement, when he says, *"You will show me the path of life; in Your presence is fullness of joy, at Your right hand there are pleasures forevermore."*[2]

The sad sack faces of people who do not have any relationship with their Lord, or who are merely religious,

---

[1] Neh 8:10
2. Psalm 16:11
3. Psalm 23:5-6

have become the main reason why the outside world would not have anything to do with us.

"No Sir," is the cry of my spirit. "Whatever He has planned for me, I want every drop of it. The Bible says, *"he prepares for me a table in the presence of my enemies,* and also, *"Surely goodness and mercy shall follow me, all the days of my life."*[1]

Faith

There are some speeches, which could not be made by ordinary men. As soon as you hear them, you feel that there is a ring about them that is by no means common.

Certain expressions which have been heard and remembered could have been uttered only by great warriors, or by men who have navigated the vast ocean. Only those who have had to fight with spiritual foes, or have done business on the great waters of soul trouble could, have uttered certain other still nobler expressions.

When you hear the expression, *"If there are as many devils at Worms as there are tiles on the housetops, I will go there in God's name,"* you are quite certain the speaker is Martin Luther. No other than he could have said it.

Faith is not something, you generate. Mortal man is incapable of understanding faith, but when our Lord indwells us, faith comes with Him as a gift. [2]

Someone once said, "The mower with the sharp scythe cuts down the grass, but he cannot touch the secret

---

[2] Eph. 2:8 (b)

source of our hope, and joy, and confidence in God, and, above all, he cannot touch the God in whom we confide."

Suddenly, your spiritual eyes are opened to understand that our Lord, is not a fantasy, but a definite reality that can and will move mountains and take you places before untouched and unseen.

Love

We are passing through the most critical period of human history. Al that has been buildt through centuries is in danger of being destroyed.

Is there a remedy that can be applied at this dark hour that will save the situation?

Our home life is disintegrating. The whole moral structure of family life is endangered.

There is something lacking.

Natural human love has failed.

Again and again we have asked the question: "Why has it failed?"

It is because it is based upon selfishness. It has been unable to stand the tremendous test of selfishness that has been developed by modern education.

There is a combat that is touching every life. It is the war between Natural Love and Selfishness, and love is losing he fight. You see it in the Divorce Court, in the struggle between Capital and Labor, between the classes.

Has God a solution for this problem?

Yes, He has.

It is a Love that is overlooked by our society and impossible to be experienced by the natural man. It is a love that is common, only in the realm of the Spirituals.

You see.; Love has never given birth to a pain.

Love has never wantonly crushed or broken the tender flower of faith that rows in the heart of trust.

'Love is God, unveiled. God is love.

This love life is God actually living Himself in us as He lived in Jesus.

There was ruggedness about the Master and yet a gentle tenderness that caused children to climb up into His arms and put their hands on his face. They longed to fondle Him, to hold His hand, to be near Him.

The love that was in the Man of Galilee is the love that is to rule the Church, rule the home, and rule this heart of ours.

Love is to the human heart what flowers are to the hillside. Flowers cover the naked, rugged places in the soil. They grow around the rocks. They grow among the roots. They cover up the wounds in the earth's surface. They cover the clay and bleak soil with a garment of lorry and royalty, of lustrous beauty. So love covers the ragged rough spots in the human.

Love is the reason for the flower garden, just as love was the reason for the flowers being.

Love gathers the flowers and arranges them to please the eye and make glad the heart.

Love makes the home beautiful. Love comes and lives in the home to keep it a place of happiness.'

Love is the most beautiful thing. It may be the most frail, yet it has the most enduring strength of anything of which we know.

When man is love ruled, love owned, love motivated, he does not shrink from any sacrifice.

Love made that ugly Cross beautiful.

Love made that tomb, that darksome dreaded tomb where death held sway, beautiful

Love stripped dearth of its terror. Love made the naked, thorn-crowned Man of Galilee the King of Lonely Heart.

My heart calls Him the Naked King of the storm tossed, broken Human.

Love made me crown Him, not with thorns, but with my heart-its devotion.

Love drives that delicate tender spirit into the darkest heathenism of Africa to endure every privation, to be shut alone with heathen minds that have no sense of appreciation, not touch of love, just cold indifference and selfish greed, and yet that love spirit lives and thrives and pours itself out until that dark place blossoms with all the tender fragrance of the New Creation.[1]

"Even As"

W.W. Kenyon says that there are two little words in the New Law of the New Covenant that challenged him. He says they reached out their tender hands and gripped him.

It is the words, "Even As."

I saw the dainty tendril of a climbing vine lay its soft, frail hand upon the coarse, hard rock, and after a bit it had fastened itself to the rock.

Those two little words seem like the delicate angers of that beautiful climbing vine.

"That ye love one another even as I have loved you."

At first I tried to get away from them but they followed me, followed as only love can follow.

I could hear them in the chambers of my soul, like the memory of a long forgotten hymn that comes back and raps at the door of the heart.

I kept saying, "Even as." Then I turned and listened and said, "Even as what?"

"As I have loved you."

I said, "I can't do it Master. I can 't love like that.

---

[1] E.W. Kenyon

If I loved like that I would be obliged to give away everything I own."

Then He said so gently, "What is it that you would need to give away?

I took an inventory of the things that I felt I would have to give away if I loved "even as" He loved me.

After the inventory of the things that I felt I would have to give away if I loved "even as" He loved me, I said, "But what would I get in place of the rich treasures of mine?"

Then He showed me wealth that I had never seen before.

If Love loved even as He loved I would have His companionship. I would have His strength. I would have His gentleness, His forbearance. I would give away the toys of the Senses to get the wealth of the Spirit.

I would give away things that perish with the using to receive something that increased in the using. I saw then a joy I had never known.

"I drew them with cords of a man, with bands of love: and I was to them as they that take off the yoke on their jaws, and I laid meat unto them."[1]

Once this infallible love, this Divine ebb of God, fills your heart, you can undoubtedly join the poet when he says:

"Should earth against my soul engage,
And hellish darts be hurl'd,
Now I can smile at Satan's rage,
And face a frowning world."[2]

---

[1] Hos 11:4
[2] Unknown

The Anointing

Well meaning people come to me all the time, asking, "How may we get more of God?" The question is rather confusing, as I don't see God as coming to us in fair portions.

God in us is the same as the Father in Jesus. There is no difference. He is no less powerful in us, as what He was inside the Apostles, or any of the great men of God in the bible.

The problem is not "how can we get more of God," the question to be answered is plainly this; "How may God get more of you?"

In the first Epistle of John, he explicitly deals with this subject in detail.

Firstly he says that you may be able to test yourself if you have God in you or not. The answer is pretty straightforward according to John. He says; "you know that you love Him, *when you keep His commandments*."

You also know that you love Him when you love your brother unconditionally. Don't fool yourself. Don't be a liar, like John refers to those who live double standards. No, rather test yourself. Put yourself to the test, and come to a conclusive answer.

John says, if God lives inside us, we have an anointing. The anointing is inside us, and we know it.

That anointing is the very essence of the Spirit of God, who lives inside of us, and it is unmistakably there, or it is not there. You don't have to wonder. You know it. You know that it is there and whenever it flows through you, it is the same as when Jesus felt the "Virtue" flow out of him, after the woman with the issue of blood touched him.

This anointing is substance. It is not a mere theory of someone's doctrinal convictions. It is real and it is a force and a weapon in the hand of the believer that leads us with eyes of the spirit in this spiritual realm.

When it is inside someone, you see it. You'll see it when they sing, you'll see it when they laugh, and you will see it when they talk about this life in the spirit realm.

This anointing also leads and directs. It brings the unknown to your spirit and gives understanding to an otherwise, ignorant, human intelligence.

Once, while I was standing at a red light in the downtown of Johannesburg, waiting to cross to the other side, after the light would turn green, the anointing of God came onto my spirit. On the opposite side of the street, amongst a crowd of people standing there, was a tall man with a beard.

The Spirit of God welled up inside me, and the anointing was present to witness to the truth.

God spoke to me, telling me to speak to this tall stranger.

The only problem was that God didn't tell me what to say to him!

The light turned green and he started towards me, and as we passed each other in the middle of the street, I felt myself filled with a reluctance to obey.

The man passed me by, and as I continued forward with my stubborn pride, I felt the anointing constraining me.

God spoke to me, and said, "He will be forever lost."

Suddenly boldness came over me and I turned and ran up behind the stranger. I touched him on his shoulder and said, "Excuse me Sir!"

The man turned and looked at me with bewildered eyes. His expression was one I would not soon forget.

"What do you want?" The stranger asked me, almost barking the words out with frustration written all over me.

I was not phased out. The anointing was strong and I found myself saying to the man, "I am a Christian Sir, and I clearly heard God say to me, to speak to you."

A frown formed on his face, and with a renewed interest he asked, "What did He say?"

I felt my heart drop into my shoes. I could see that the next few words would make or break a situation for this frustrated human being. I did not know him, but I could see desperation written over his face. I was hoping that some eloquent sentence would come over my lips. Some real revelation of sorts, but as I opened my mouth to speak, the Holy Spirit filled my mouth with a very simple statement.

"God said, I must tell you to give Jesus a chance!" I was disappointed in myself. I thought, "I could have done better than that," when I noticed the man's countenance change. His eyes opened wide and like a hungry child he leaned forward for another portion.

"Did He really say that?" The stranger asked.

Suddenly, I came to a full realization that God was at work through me. The anointing was flowing like a force through me, and all I could do was to nod in agreement.

The stranger started crying. Tears flowed over his cheeks and after getting his composure back he told me that he had just returned from the divorce court where his wife left him for another man and his children was taken from him. He told me briefly that he had been declared bankrupt, and then he said, "I was on my way home, and I was going to take my shotgun and blow my brains out!"

My head literally spun as I realized that God used me to stop this stranger in his tracks with a simple offer, "Give Jesus a chance!"

"Hallelujah," how can a person exchange eternal moments like those for the wealth of the temporal realm of mere mortality?

Time stood still for the stranger and I when we knelt down in the middle of Johannesburg, as I introduced him to my friend, and Creator, Jesus, the Peacemaker.

Many a believer have stories and greater than these to tell, only because they learned to yield to the call of God, through the anointing of the Holy Spirit.

> *"Anointing fall on me, anointing fall on me*
> *Let the Spirit of the Holy Ghost fall on me,*
> *Anointing, fall on me."*

For More books from Yan Venter, contact Amazon.com or go to his Website at: yanventer.net